The

CHICKEN WHISPERER

A TRUE STORY

BY TIMM HAMMER JONSON

The CHICKEN WHISPERER
A TRUE STORY

BY TIMOTHY HAMMER JONSON

In Memory of
Tara Stover

In Honor of
Brenda Knipper

With hopes for Terry, Chris, Whitney, Jenny, Laura, C.M., Kristie, Nikki, April, Keli, and the many other flowers in the garden of my life.

TABLE OF CONTENTS

PREFACE

I decided to write this book knowing that "I" might actually be the person it helps. When I looked at the first part of my life, quite frankly, I was disappointed with the quality of my relationships, and I knew it was my own fault.

I also knew if the second half of my life was going to be any better, I was going to have to look at what might be wrong with me, because the only the thing we really have the power to change is ourselves.

Like a lost man stumbling across a desert seeking water, I began a desperate search for answers. I found my thirst quenched in the most unusual place. It was in a book I found in my attic while dealing with a giant squirrel.

This author, who I refer to as the Chicken Whisperer, told an incredible story of loving someone who struggled to love him back. Later, in an attempt to show his love for this person, he lost his life. But his story, unbelievably, is still very much alive.

A lot of books claim to have all the answers, but none really do—except for the book I found in my attic. For me the challenge is no longer where to find what I have been looking for, but rather what to do with it now that I have found it.

The Chicken Whisperer's dying wish was that we would honor him by sharing his secrets about better relationships. Sharing what I learned is the least I can do. Ultimately, I want to become just like him.

A command from God is a whisper, a soft scream to the heart that is wandering in the wrong direction.

"Bring... bring it home? All right, let's bring it home. If you was hit by a truck and you was lying out there in that gutter dying, and you had time to sing one song. Huh? One song that people would remember before you're dirt. One song that would let God know how you felt about your time here on Earth. One song that would sum you up. You tellin' me that's the song you'd sing? That same Jimmy Davis tune we hear on the radio all day, about your peace within, and how it's real, and how you're gonna shout it? Or... would you sing somethin' different, somethin' real, Somethin' *you* feel? Cause I'm telling you right now, that's the kind of song people want to hear. That's the kind of song that truly saves people."

...from the movie Walk the Line

LAVA SOAP SHOWER

I was interrupted watching *Walk the Line* by the deafening screech of a twenty-year-old smoke alarm. Gently setting my Mountain Dew can down beside my bed, I flew downstairs into a thick cloud of black smoke. Stumbling into the kitchen, I found my chicken tenders in flames and my stove melting. Unfortunately, my brave attempt at turning the stove off was thwarted by hot, smoking buttons. All I could think about was how I wished I had hit record on my Tivo.

Flames out, covered in soot, and looking like a coal miner at the end of a twelve-hour shift, I began to survey the damage. The tiny flames didn't do anything other than melt a few plastic knobs. The smoke, on the other hand, made three rooms look like somebody shot off a black powder cannon in my house. With my lungs full of ash, looking at my blackened, recently renovated hundred-year old house, all I could think about was how I was wasting my life, again.

Thoreau wrote, *"You can't kill time without injuring eternity."* He also said he didn't want to get to the end of his life and figure out he had never really lived. *"I went to the woods because I wished to live deliberately, to front only the essential facts of life, and see if I could not learn what it had to teach, and not, when I came to die, discover that I had not lived."* So his solution was to undergo an experiment and remove the distractions. In an effort to reduce his life to its simplest terms, he built an isolated one-room cabin by Walden Pond and called it home for a couple of years.

I have no desire to abandon all the comforts of life (morning lattes and Tivo) for a shack in the woods, but I do share Thoreau's fear of being easily distracted by remodeling projects and other tedious, time-consuming tasks. To be honest, my life often resembles the character Randy (Ralphie's little brother in the movie *A Christmas Story*) who is over dressed by his mother for a cold snowy day: constrained, hidden, rendered incapacitated by the good intentions of impressing a world of people who aren't really watching.

Like Thoreau, I guess I need to simplify. I need to focus on the *"essential facts of life."* But I'm not moving to Alaska; I'm not building a one-room cabin; and I'm not going to write metaphorically about squirrels and ponds. Instead I am going to write a book about what I believe really matters: developing deeper and more meaningful relationships in my life, with God and with people.

And I will be learning as I go. I have an idea that most of what I need to know I have already learned along the way. And it is just a matter of digging it up. Like my raw passion, my childlike sense of wonder, and my risky faith, I've lost the essential facts of life along the way. And I've learned the best way to find something you've lost is to go back to where you were when you remember having it.

So maybe if I get hit by a truck, I'll be working on something real, something valuable, the kind of thing that "truly saves people," even myself. But first I'm going to take a shower with Lava soap because I look like I crawled through a chimney, and then go get a Big Mac because I'm still hungry.

HAMMER vs. GODZILLA

A l Gore will tell you global warming is being caused by years of pollution thickening the earth's atmosphere, creating a greenhouse effect. I will tell you Al Gore is wrong. It is directly linked to a thirty-pound squirrel living in my attic. (I guess I am breaking my promise about not talking about squirrels.)

On a cold February day, prior to my chicken tender fire, I went to my mailbox looking for a random love letter from a beautiful woman and found a $700 gas bill. Now either I was grilling a lot of steaks, was growing a rainforest in my basement, or was heating a winter pool I'd never seen. I started looking around for the pool but found my problem in my attic.

My attic door looked like something out of the movie The Grudge. The prior tenants used eight cans of foam sealant around it trying to keep cold air, and whatever else was up there, from coming down into the house. The door was also full of nails, screws, and strangely, a few teeth marks in the dry rotted foam. All attempts at keeping it closed had failed. It was standing half open.

Because of this, my house had basically become a giant chimney. Heat escaped for weeks causing the trees in my yard to bud in

January and the bearings in my gas meter to burn out. What was sad is that while I was warm and asleep dreaming about *Celtic Women* in concert, a furry version of Godzilla was running around my attic enjoying his own seventy-two degree living space.

After I gathered up enough courage to go exploring, I found both eave vents were open and unprotected because the screens covering them had holes in them the size of softballs. Something big with sharp teeth had chewed through the metal. I sensed it wasn't a shark.

A few days later, when I was back in the attic repairing the holes, I found my culprit. While I was climbing over abandoned books and boxes of photographs my flashlight caught a glimpse of a fur coat in the corner. I squinted and realized the coat had a tail, and it was twitching. Less than fifteen feet away from me, staring at me like I was supper, was a squirrel I named Godzilla.

I named him Godzilla because he looked at me like I was a building he was about to crush. He was huge, a freak of nature, a pro wrestler in squirrel world. A shotgun would have just ticked him off. Pinned in, he knew the only way out was to chew through my newly installed screen in ten seconds or kill a man. I could tell by the glare in his glassy black eyes he knew it was easier to kill a man.

My frog gigging experience told me to keep a light on him, and he wouldn't move. My life experience told me holding a light on a giant squirrel is like trying to kill an elephant with a toothpick. I knew within seconds he would be gnawing on my neck and choking me with his tail. I did what anyone who had seconds to live would do: I talked my way out of it.

I started telling him how I forgave him for putting me in financial distress. I told him he had nice, strong white teeth and should think about doing a Crest commercial. I said if I believed in reincarnation I would definitely come back as his species because I thought it was cool how he could fly from tree to tree and live on a diet of nuts. I mentioned I was impressed with how he could remember where he hid those nuts. And the whole time I was talking I was tip toeing my way over to the screen I had just fixed. As a gesture of sincerity, I removed it while reminding him how much I enjoyed watching Rocky and Bullwinkle as a kid, but I also always thought the squirrel was so much smarter than the moose. Then, while I retreated, Godzilla pardoned me and crawled out of my world back into his.

As I slowly made my way back to the door with a flashlight in hand, I climbed over box after box of ancient photographs. I dodged a child's bent train track, his dirty one-eyed plush polar bear, and his dusty wooden case of Lincoln logs. I realized that one day my things would lie around in an attic covered in dust and wondered exactly what kind of legacy I would leave behind. And it was at this moment I noticed a book lying under an air conditioning duct, a book, unbelievably, I had read before. I opened it and began reacquainting myself with the author who had written an incredible love story with aspirations to become a Chicken Whisperer. It was this book that prompted me to approach my problem with his incredible wisdom about relationships, to apply his ancient love secrets to my life, and, as he encourages, to begin the process by reconnecting with my childhood.

Of course all of our lives are shaped by our childhood, and mine was full of surprises. Like a small shift in the ocean floor can create a wave that wipes out an entire island chain, small serious moments interrupted my younger years and abruptly changed the landscape of my heart. At the time I did not find these life lessons funny or helpful, but in reflection I cannot help but laugh and be thankful. Time has a way of taking our wounds and reconciling them to the "essential facts" of our life.

Like an attic, my childhood was interesting, mysterious, and intimidating. Sometimes there was a fight, and sometimes there was a kiss, but rarely both at the same moment. There was family. There were friends. And yes, there were monsters.

I know that great life stories are about people like Napoleon, Alexander the Great, and Spartacus who gained power through fighting; and about people like Joan of Arc, Jesus Christ, and Martin Luther King, Jr. who gained power through dying. I know that great life stories are also about people like Romeo & Juliet, Mark Anthony & Cleopatra, and Sampson & Delilah, who took great risk for romance ... with tragic endings (one drank poison, three fell on sharp objects, and one was crushed to death). But often the more we risk, even though it puts us in peril, it also puts us in a position to find the life we were meant to live.

I have rarely played it safe. I have often taken risks. I have made many mistakes. Whether my life is a great love story with a happy ending or a classic romantic tragedy remains to be seen, because it is far from finished. But one thing is clear: I have already been loved by great people. Through the mutual experience of our lives these people have imparted to me the priceless foundational wisdom of loving someone other than myself. And, this wisdom started in childhood.

IN THE BEGINNING

Delivery is like trying to push a watermelon through a Cheerio. I, an extra large melon, squeezed my way into the world on a Monday. A nurse rinsed off my body, wrapped me up like a burrito, and handed me to my mother. I've been hungry ever since.

A lot was going on in 1969. As the last issue of *The Saturday Evening Post* was rolling off the press, the first Boeing 747 was taking off. While Neil Armstrong was taking one giant leap for mankind, Wal-Mart was taking its first baby step as a corporation. Woodstock was rocking out New York and Hurricane Camille was slamming Mississippi. As Judy Garland was saying goodbye, I was saying hello.

I was born with three hundred and fifty bones and soft knees (they don't harden until we start walking). I had no teeth or hair and every woman who saw me thought I was attractive. I am now on my second full set of teeth (the first one fell out when I was seven), I have a full head of hair, and my knees are as hard as diamonds. What happened to all the women who found me attractive?

I was the third in a series of children. I was also the last. From this point forward we were a family of five growing up on a rustic dairy farm in West Tennessee. With my arrival, my mother left her teaching job and my father signed up for full time fire fighting. He must have had a premonition I would love to play with matches.

Out my back door was a garden where plants grew and insects feasted. I was surrounded by interesting neighbors who had interesting hobbies and sheds full of great ideas. One mile from my house was a church, the one I would grow up in. Two miles from my house was a country store, the one I would walk to. And three miles from my house was a lake, the one I would fish in. All three places would become my sanctuaries.

I didn't know it then, but I know it now; my childhood was the best part of my life. Herbert Gold wrote, "*He carried his childhood like a hurt warm bird held to his middle-aged breast.*" I feel like that; I love those fragile small years of my life when my heart was still fresh enough to fall completely and totally in love with a turtle; when my faith was young enough to pray as if I always believed someone was really listening; and when I was crazy enough to trust people, even myself.

My childhood was far from perfect, but it was an exceptional human experience. There were skinned knees and bloody lips, bee stings and rotten apples, black eyes and dead pets, but there was also enough love to bind my wounds. It wasn't that long ago, but in terms of how important it was to me, it will always be forever.

And it is here where I must return if I am to find what I am looking for. The Chicken Whisperer said in order to become who we want to be we must reclaim the heart of a child, reduce the moon to cheese and hunt for the unicorn. We must restore our faith in once upon a time and happily ever after. We must become like a child.

If the following stories seem a bit random, bear with me as I ramble through the attic of my life. However petty it seems, it was this process of discovery that ultimately brought my heart to its knees, and this is where I found what I was looking for.

Sometimes the heart needs to reacquaint itself with the past to prepare it for it's future. Yet I also understand the past can be a scary place for some who painfully suffered during their early years of life. To you, I say hold my hand and follow me. Trust me, this is a journey we both need to take.

FRANK & FLOSSIE

Most people do not recognize the name Larry Walters. And even fewer people witnessed the event that made him famous. On July 2, 1982 he took forty-five weather balloons, filled them with helium, tied them to a lawn chair, and with a pellet gun in his hand, soared three miles up into history as an American adventurer. After about forty-five minutes he descended safely into power lines causing a temporary blackout in Long Beach. When asked by a reporter why he did it, he replied, *"A man can't just sit around."*

Larry Walters reminds me of my grandfather, a man who didn't believe in sitting around but believed in making sure everyone else did. My grandfather repaired lawn chairs.

Frank Silkwood's typical day started with an electric razor shave, a little splash of Old Spice, and buttered toast with jelly. From there, he walked out to his leaning garage, picked out a few aluminum lawn chairs in need of repair, gathered up a few rolls of nylon ribbon, and, under a canopy of plastic flowers, he mended the broken.

Why he collected plastic flowers I'm not sure. It looked like he had robbed a graveyard, but more than likely he was saving the ones that had been discarded. I guess I should have wondered more about where he got all those broken lawn chairs. Maybe he had a secret wrestling fetish?

Going to visit my grandparents in Illinois was the equivalent of the Pilgrim's Mayflower voyage. My parents believed the eleventh commandment was *"Thou shalt not break the speed limit."* The speed limit was 30, 45, and 55mph in the early seventies. I could have ridden my bike faster. I think we left the day after Thanksgiving to arrive on Christmas. My mother packed fresh fruit to fend off scurvy. But the voyage was worth it.

Frank and Flossie's hearts were softened on the hard anvil of mental illness. Two of their children were diagnosed with schizophrenia. Their relentless love for these children took them on a journey that transformed them into powerful loving people. Not until I was much older did I discover that my uncle Kyle's illness was often a public affair. He once ran nude through the local cemetery with a butcher knife claiming God had called him to castrate himself. Never once did I detect regret or anger in my loving grandparents about having adult children who in a way never grew up. Actually, their love and treatment of Kyle allowed him to become a talented storyteller medicated with sweet tea and cigarettes. He entertained me for hours with tales about the world, interrupted only by smoke rings. And he taught me how to drive a car with repeated short trips to Hungry Jacks.

When I visited, Frankie would fiddle with a few chairs and then peek into the kitchen to tell Flossie he was taking the *"Grands"* to get

20

some candy. She would respond by saying, "*It's awfully close to lunch time*" or "*You're going to rot their teeth out.*" By the time she got the words out of her mouth we were already a block away.

He took us a short distance to a little grocery store called Spontak's where the best selling items were loaf bologna, cartons of cigarettes, and nickel candy. I didn't smoke and ate more bologna than a kid in the great depression so I gravitated toward the candy. With a quarter Frankie gave me, I tapped on the thick glass case to indicate my choices. Usually I got a handful of *Sixlets*, a few *Now & Laters*, a couple of *Laffy Taffy*, and a *Chick-A-Stick*. I felt like my transaction was the most important event that would ever take place in my lifetime, kind of like buying a house. The neat thing was Mr. Spontak acted the same way.

On the way back we usually took a different route home and crossed a few bridges where we ran from trolls and the Loch Ness monster. Skipping, we made a few wishes, threw a few rocks, and ate all our candy. Our time was always wrapped in laughter.

Another great thing about visiting Frankie was late at night when Flossie turned in he would take us to the kitchen, pull out a loaf of bread, and make us all buttered toast and jelly. Before we destroyed the evidence, a disappointed Flossie would appear in a pink housecoat and say, "*Frankie you're going to spoil these kids.*" Frankie would say, "*That's the plan.*"

I still remember hearing Frankie was sick. A few weeks later, we got into the van and headed north for his funeral. I was only six. I

21

knew my colors, my numbers, and my alphabet, but I remember being scared, scared of what I didn't know. Death was something that happened to flowers, mosquitoes and fish. It never really occurred to me that it would happen to all of us.

I remember walking into the funeral home and seeing a bunch of dressed up people, half smiling, half crying, reminiscing and struggling to accept there would be no new stories. It felt like a birthday party with bad cake. Frankie was lying in a casket with his arms folded across his chest, his face turned toward Heaven. He was cradled in gray silk against a background of pink roses. I was too scared, but I wanted to touch him as I thought back to the garage where he mended chairs under a canopy of flowers, to the bridge where he made me laugh, and to the kitchen were he spoiled me. I cried not only because I lost somebody I loved, but even more because I lost somebody who loved me.

He was born before the airplane but lived to see Neil Armstrong walk on the moon. He was born before the Model-T Ford but lived long enough to own a Lincoln Continental. He weathered the Great Depression and two world wars. He survived the Orient No. 2 coal-mine disaster and the Tri-state tornado of 1925. He appears to have been here at a great period in history, yet he made me feel like I was the only thing he was ever really waiting for.

During these seven years of my life this seventy year old man taught me hundreds of things about being a kid, and one important thing about childhood: when we lose something we love, we cry; and when we lose someone we love, we weep.

22

*"Did I ever tell you about the oysters? **Oysters?** I didn't tell you bout the oysters? Think about all the millions of oysters lying around on the bottom of the ocean. Then one day, God comes along and he says, "I think I'm gonna make that one different," and you know what he does? He puts a little piece of sand in it. And guess what it can do that the others can't. **What?** It can make a beautiful pearl."*

...from the movie Fried Green Tomatoes

PARENTS & PEARLS

S lavery didn't end with the Civil War: we all have parents. I'm not suggesting that all parent's view kids as property but a few have the idea that for a kid to make it in the world today their capacity for work must be tested.

Whereas most kids began boot camp with the simple task of keeping their room clean, my training began deep in a small jungle called a garden. Within this two thousand square foot torture chamber we grew our groceries.

The boot camp was rarely fenced, save a rare electric wire during the years when rabbits were plentiful. To simply keep me at the task of pulling weeds my mother, with switch in hand, sternly warned me that there would be no mercy if the job was not complete by high noon. Our reward was to shuck corn and shell purple hull peas in the shade. I was spoiled.

At times, when morale in the camp was low, my mother would load my two sisters and I into our green car where our bare legs would burn on hot vinyl seats while we drove two miles down the road to Manley's store. She would give each of us a quarter and let us stick our head in the cooler to look for the coldest RC soda we could find. We'd grab a Chick-A-Stick or a Zero Bar and zip back home to mass production.

Even while trying to catch an episode of *Love Boat* on a Saturday night, a bowl of green beans to be snapped was placed in my lap to help me relax. I really liked television but my fingers were always too sore to applaud any genius in script writing. I was basically held hostage by vegetables.

I favored watermelon. This king of the garden required very little care and just one of these giants equaled all the blackberries I could pick in a lifetime. There was also some sinful satisfaction in the fact I got to take the biggest knife in the kitchen and sink it into its pink flesh. This green giant was my therapy for a childhood of imprisonment.

It should be no surprise I picked my nose as a kid because I was trained to pick: pick strawberries, pick tomatoes, pick cucumbers, pick apples, pick blackberries, pick okra, and pick ticks off my flesh. I was a picker and proud of it.

But in spite of all the sunburns, all the sore fingernails, all the blood lost to ticks, I found something growing in that garden I did not expect to find... a respect for my owners (parents).

James would come home after ten hours of hard labor and pull an antique garden tiller out of the shed that would never start. After a few pokes with a screwdriver and a can of starting fluid, it would crackle to life, breathing smoke like a dragon. Tilling a garden is like trying to make an alligator eat your grass in straight rows while holding its tail without getting bitten. It requires forearms like Popeye and determination like Wiley Coyote. With the July sun beating down on his sweating forehead, my father did something he didn't love to do, fighting and struggling with the machine each and every step. Like a knight he went into the cave, but rather than slay the dragon, he trained it. This important summer lesson taught me to fight, even when you don't feel like it, because other people are usually counting on you to bring home the bacon, or at least the tomatoes and lettuce to go with it.

A few minutes later we'd all sit down and have a five- course meal. Beverly's commitment to vegetables was unmatched. She would plant them, water them, pick them, shuck them, cook them, cut them, bag them, freeze them, un-thaw them, and cook them again. I once heard in the battle between the rock and stream, the stream always wins, not by strength but by persistence. My mother was a stream, at times water torture, who taught me if you finish what you start you won't go hungry.

In a way parents are like a piece of sand in our life's shell, an annoying intrusion that in retrospect is the most beautiful thing that ever happens to us. Through discipline and tough love they prepare us for the art of being faithful in long-term relationships. They teach

25

us the thorn is part of the rose and the race is part of the victory. Our parents, like God, teach us sometimes loving someone involves bleeding on their behalf... sometimes even when they're the ones causing us the injury.

My parents were patient; my parents were forgiving; and my parents were hell bent on making sure I didn't go there. Their plan was simple: put Timmy in the garden and make him eat his vegetables and pray, pray that he understands that for anything in life to taste good you not only have to understand where it comes from but also what it cost to get it on your plate. And hopefully he'll understand that bad taste in his mouth, that sand of tough love, is producing something in him that will be regarded by those who love him later in life as sacred.

Davidge: [after Jerry saved Davidge from a sand monster] You saved my life. Why?
Jerry: Maybe I need to look at another face... even one as ugly as yours.
Davidge: So you still think humans are ugly?
Jerry: Compared to a Drac? VERY ugly. But that thing out there... is even more ugly than you

....from the movie Enemy Mine

DANCING WITH A CURLING IRON

A bathroom is where a man brushes his teeth, gets rid of a little processed food and liquids, and takes a bath. A bathroom is where a woman cuts her nails, shaves her legs, takes a bath, brushes her teeth, cleans her face, plucks her brows, applies her makeup, curls her hair, and sprays her perfume. It is a woman's territory guarded by a curling iron.

Siblings have been fighting each other since Cain killed Abel. History has a record of siblings struggling to coexist--- Jacob and Esau, Leah and Rachel, Raymond and Robert Barone. The idea of introducing weapons into the mix probably didn't take long especially with guys like Joseph getting pretty jackets. Although it does appear the experience gained while using weapons to beat siblings prepared people for greater things. Just look at David, he threw a few rocks and it completely changed his life. I thought with two sisters I would definitely need some equipment, so I started with an iron fire poker.

With sisters there is one war but many battles. A typical battle was fighting over who stood in front of our fireplace. During the seventies in the rural south fireplaces were not a place for candles or decorative gas logs, instead they were full of real burning wood failing miserably at what it was intended to do: produce heat. To compensate for its lack of enthusiasm we stood directly in front of the flames and let our pajama bottoms start smoking before we spun around to burn the opposite side. With very little room available for individual roasting, a battle for the key positions typically ensued.

After a particularly cold January night I arrived at the fireplace first to knock off the morning chill but was bumped out of the way to freeze to death by two older sisters. Teeth chattering and approaching hypothermic shock in my thin Denver Broncos pajama suit, I surveyed the situation and saw help standing in the corner.

Leaning against the wall was my weapon of choice, a nice long, skinny, iron fire poker weighing about four pounds. I quietly backed to the corner and wrapped my hands around the shaft as if I was preparing to hit a golf ball four hundred yards. I then strolled to my previous source of warmth and struck my youngest sister across both shins (I learned to attack the smaller one from watching the Animal Kingdom), immediately freeing up space in front of the fireplace. Desperate situations require desperate measures.

Don't worry; I got more than I dished out. Chris, the small one and a chemist, had an obsession with cats while growing up and collected toy Garfields. Terry, the accountant, was too busy reading romance novels and didn't learn to drive until her senior year of college. Between one collecting stuffed animals and the other collecting Harlequin Romance stories my sisters still found time to crush my hands with a cellar door, rub red peppers on my face, and jam my front teeth half way into my gums. Thanks to them I developed a high tolerance for cats, books with funny pictures on the cover, pain, and the sight of my own blood.

Another common battle was a familiar one called "calling shotgun" which originates from bank robberies where the best shooter rode opposite the driver in the getaway car to shoot at the police. Whether we were going to the grocery store to get Cheerios or to church to get a helping of grace, we always fought over who would ride shotgun.

Sitting in the front seat made me feel superior to the girls in the back. Of course I usually had to forget a female was driving and that rich people almost always sit in the back, but so do prisoners. At the time it simply meant I had won a battle in a war I felt like I was losing. In reflection it was poor planning. Never turn your back on the enemy.

I have a reputation of falling asleep while riding in a vehicle; I think in part because my mother mowed the grass while she was pregnant and I still find motor vibrations soothing. Regardless of why, my sisters waited about two minutes for me to nod off with my mouth wide open and started poking all sorts of stuff in my pie hole. I usually woke up and looked in the mirror to find a couple of pieces of gum on my forehead, an old straw in my mouth, and a bright color of lipstick on my lips. Never turn your back on the enemy, especially with your mouth wide open.

We all know the biggest battle between siblings is actually the battle for attention. Big battles call for great weapons, weapons like faking your own death.

When you're in a garden with two sisters the natural thing to do is throw something, a pepper, a strawberry, a tomato, something, anything. And the goal is to get hit with what taste good.

What started out as a friendly game of tossing rotten cucumbers one day quickly escalated into an attempt to blind each other with dirt-clods. Of course being younger and out numbered, it wasn't long before I felt like I was dying in a dusty hailstorm. Feeling defeated, I said the magic word, "timeout," and was running out of the garden toward the house when I felt the impact.

A large dirt clod the size of an apple, traveling in excess of 40mph, struck my head. My first thought was, "#$%!, *that hurt!*" My second thought was, "*This is my acting debut.*" In a cloud of dust I simply fell face forward and proceeded to act as if I was dead, killed by a dirt clod.

Their initial laughter was soon replaced by the silence of the reality that they, just like Cain, had just murdered their only brother. They quietly tiptoed over calling my name while I remained motionless, milking the moment for all its glory. Then with tears

30

forming in their eyes they gently shook my limp body with no response. Realizing it was a serious situation they bolted for the kitchen screaming, *"We killed Timmy! We killed Timmy!"* trying to retrieve my mother. Meanwhile, enjoying the smell of freshly cut grass, I remained face down waiting to be surrounded by three women all mourning the loss of the omega male in the family.

Faking your death as a child has three huge advantages. First it clarifies that your family really does care, or at least enough to cry over your corpse. Second, to emerge from death is easy; you simply pretend you were unconscious. And third, you usually get special treatment for your nonexistent symptoms of head trauma, special treatment like Coke and ice cream.

But whatever advantage I gained through swinging fire pokers, calling shotgun, and faking funerals, I slowly lost every morning to the burning sting of a hot curling iron. Whether every touch was intentional or accidental I'm not sure, but I am sure of one thing: it taught me to dance. Stick a piece of hot metal to an uncoordinated boy's neck and he'll turn into James Brown.

Three people trying to get ready for school in an eight by ten foot bathroom is like three squirrels on a coke can floating down the river fighting over an acorn: somebody's gonna get wet. I simply wanted to brush my teeth and splash on a little green stuff called Polo, yet this required me crawling through a demilitarized zone of curling irons to get to the sink. I paid the price more than once. I learned you never get between a girl and her mirror just like you never get between a bear and his honey tree.

31

My experience on the battlefield of the bathroom taught me something more important, that the human race has the capacity for forgiveness and a greater need to receive it. I can't explain it, but I loved, and still love, the only two girls I've ever hit: my sisters. Forgiveness enables sinful people to coexist not only with God but also with each other. The ability to say, "*my love for you is greater than your sin against me,*" sets the stage for meaningful relationships in our lives.

The Chicken Whisperer believed forgiveness was crucial to love. He believed resentment in our hearts toward one person interfered with our interactions with other people in our lives, even God. An angry man has a hard time enjoying a good dinner even if the food is great. He also believed a position of neutrality toward people who wrong us was not the solution, but rather we should kiss people who touch our necks with curling irons. The alternative of beating people up for revenge only magnifies the relational problem, or widens the gap. The Chicken Whisperer believed that we should build bridges, not burn them. Humanity is an ocean comprised of isolated islands of individuals who are separated by a gap of selfishness. And in God's genius, He put a little bit of what we need on each other's island. So the map to fulfillment becomes a relational one, a path that takes us into each other's lives. Forgiveness enables not only more access to other people, but it also makes our own shores more attractive. Without forgiveness we become self-centered and stranded in a sea of separation.

But perhaps the best thing the Chicken Whisperer said about forgiveness was that horribly sinful people who experience forgiveness have the potential to be transformed into incredible loving people by the act of grace. He said by refusing to forgive someone we are withholding something they need that is more valuable than oxygen, and there is no benefit to either one of us. When we forgive, we reduce the potential for conflict, and build a bridge for more than reconciliation; we build a bridge for a potential meaningful relationship in not only our lives but in theirs as well.

The Chicken Whisperer said that it was silly to expect mercy if we ourselves fail to extend mercy to those who offend us. He said children are great examples of how to tweak these rare relational qualities. Just watch how siblings can crack a coke bottle on each other's head, push each other off the monkey bars, or stick gum in each other's hair and amazingly overcome these transgressions within minutes. Children probably understand in all likelihood it will happen again but the alternative of having no one to play with is even worse. Their awareness of their need for community overrides their desire for a sterile protective environment. They take the risk because the reward is worth it.

I think one thing we all miss about our own childhood is that good night of sleep when there was no axe to grind, no revenge to seek, no ill will toward anyone: a time when we were building bridges not burning them. Maybe a good night's sleep is what we need? Maybe in order to do that, we need to forgive some people? Maybe we need to ask some people to forgive us?

Louise Jefferson: Lionel, you'd better go to your room. I don't want you to get hit by your father.

Lionel Jefferson: Why would Dad hit me?

Louise Jefferson: Because I'm not sure just where I'm going to throw him!

WILMA, WEESY & A WOOLY MAMMOTH

I didn't have the World Wide Web growing up in the seventies & eighties, but I still had www: Wilma, Weesy, and a wooly mammoth. Five fuzzy channels taught me a lot about relationships.

In the seventies on the farm there was no cable, no satellite dish, and no remote control. There was a thing called an antenna that needed fairly constant adjustment and another thing called a dial that tuned in five channels. I watched my limited world of television in black and white until 1977 when my dad brought home a used color TV. It was missing the back cover and could have killed anyone brave enough to make an adjustment. We just consented to watching everything in a strange hue of red, but regardless of the color, it slowly introduced me to a whole new world of thinking.

Sesame Street taught me a beautiful community of diversity is possible. By watching Big Bird (a giant yellow bird), Oscar the Grouch (a green monster), Cookie Monster (a blue monster), Count (a vampire), and Snuffaluffagus (a wooly mammoth) all get along I learned different personalities can peacefully coexist as long as they have neat songs to sing. Even Coca- Cola believed the answer to world peace was simply to *"teach the world to sing."* Naturally I assumed singing would also help me get along better with my unruly neighbors but unfortunately I chose *Paper Roses* by Marie Osmond. It was also difficult to get anybody excited about the letter K and the number 8.

The Flintstones taught me that some families are comprised of men who scream and good-looking women who tolerate them. These screaming men typically have devoted friends who also tolerate their tirades and outburst. I believed God's way of punishing Fred was to give him a car that weighed 20 tons without a motor in it and a vacuum cleaner that shed hair. I wanted to marry Wilma.

The Jefferson's taught me everybody needs a "Weesy" and nobody deserves a George. Through laughter, it taught me that sometimes the best way to approach a serious problem is to disarm everybody with a joke. I learned a lot about color watching a black and white TV.

The Brady Bunch taught me that all problems can be solved in thirty minutes. Whether it is fixing a broken nose, getting braces, finding a date, feeling left out, or someone reading your diary; life finds a way to repair itself. At first I assumed it was the maid that made everything so easy, but then it became obvious what really made the difference was Astro Turf! With no grass to mow you've got a lot of time to solve problems.

35

Andy Griffith taught me a man who smokes and plays the guitar doesn't need a gun to be a big sheriff. With a simple commitment to treating the town drunk the same as the town mayor you get a thing called respect and an aunt that cooks you fried chicken. It also taught me if you want a good mechanic make sure you find someone called Goober.

The Incredible Hulk taught me anger, if vented correctly, can actually save lives, but almost always destroys your chance at romance. A large green man running around in a shredded shirt was considered sexy in the seventies, but remember so was orange shag carpet. Shag carpet looks like real over-grown carpet with the mange.

Hee Haw taught me that those who share a love for country music usually end up telling really bad jokes in a cornfield. They also typically lie down with a dog and tell more bad jokes. However, bad jokes and good-looking girls make a fairly mesmerizing variety show.

The Love Boat taught me even rich famous people have trouble finding what they are looking for. I also learned that doctors on boats are lonely people and the smartest man on the boat is not the captain but the bartender.

Fantasy Island taught me money can't buy you happiness, even if you pay for it, although trying to buy it often sheds light on the fact you had it all along. My fantasy at the age of ten involved a truckload of Twinkies and sharing a one straw milkshake with Wilma Flintstone. I was a bad boy.

Peanuts specials taught me dogs are smarter than humans because they never let a girl hold a ball they are trying to kick. It taught me sometimes even though our mouth is moving nobody can understand us. And it also taught me it is kind of cool to wrap your whole life around protecting something small, like a yellow bird, who might eventually become your secretary and golf caddy.

Roots taught me we have some sad history in America, that war is glorified, that ironically we were once terrorists, and the truth is not always something to be proud of. It also taught me that freedom is not just something America gained from the British. It has often been something we have gained from ourselves.

But perhaps what taught me the most about people on television was simply the six o'clock news. At first I thought people were simply obsessed with bad news, that people run to watch houses burn, that people watch races to see crashes, that people watch the news to watch destruction. I thought in some twisted way it made people feel better about themselves to know it didn't happen to them, almost a sense of comfort that fate skipped their house and landed on their neighbor. And there is some truth to that. But I think more than anything we like to watch people crawl out of burning houses and mangled cars; we like to watch people survive; because like a rainbow giving us hope after the storm, these wounded survivors remind us that in the face of our own problem-ridden life we are blessed; blessed with a survival instinct, the ability

37

to push aside all those things we can't live without and focus on the one thing that really matters. We witness these moments of salvation and we begin to understand our problems are small, like braces and bloody noses; our search for love is in common places, like on boats and islands; and that under the most unusual circumstances, like living in a junkyard or living in a doghouse; with the most unusual people, like a green grouch or a green man; this instinct inside of us not only has the capacity to rescue our hearts, but to revive our ability to love as well.

"Our mission was called 'a successful failure,' in that we returned safely but never made it to the moon. In the following months it was determined that a damaged coil built inside the oxygen tank sparked during our cryo stir and caused the explosion that crippled the Odyssey. It was a minor defect that occurred two years before I was even named the flight's commander. And as for me, the seven extraordinary days of Apollo 13 were my last in space...I watched other men walk on the moon and return safely all from the confines of Mission Control and our house in Houston. I sometimes catch myself looking up at the moon remembering the changes of fortune in our long voyage, thinking of the thousands of people who worked to bring the three of us home. I look up at the moon and wonder, when will we be going back? And who will that be?"

...from the movie Apollo 13

A SUCCESSFUL FAILURE

My mom, Joan of Arc, is a northern girl married to a southern man, Timex. It would be very funny to say their marriage was like a tiny version of the civil war but it wasn't. I can only remember a couple of fights, and one of those put all of us in sleeping bags.

Camping was a compromise between my father and mother after my dad had spent a few too many evenings hitting a softball and was confronted about spending more time with the family. The man worked two hundred hours a week. A weekend of camping helped him relax as much as a weekend of re-roofing the house.

Camping is where you leave the comforts of home (television & toilet paper) to rediscover how a battery operated radio works and how pine cones have multiple uses. Sort of what the pilgrims did, except they did it to escape persecution and taxes. They also almost all died the first winter (hint, hint).

Camping, in spite of its reputation, has several advantages. First, it increases your appreciation of food (takes hours to cook) and cold soda (because the sun is usually hotter than Hades). Second, it gives you a fond affection of shelter, even if it is a musty, damp tent (anything to get away from the mosquitoes). Third, it teaches you to honor warnings about flammable clothing (never wear a sweater around a campfire, or if you do, just speed up the inevitable and soak it in gasoline).

To understand camping you divide it into two parts: what the adults do and what the kids do. The adults spend all week planning for the weekend (they usually forget something important like ketchup). Kids spend all week dreaming about the weekend. Upon arrival, adults construct a small city of canvas. Kids suffer a hearing loss and run towards water. Adults start the fire. Kids play in the fire. Adults cook the meals. Kids eat the meals. Adults apply first-aid. Kids get hurt. It's a beautiful relationship.

Ninety percent of my family's camping weekends simply involved loading the clan into a 1971 Dodge van and driving a short three miles through our farm to the family lake. Immediately, Chris and I would jump out and start making a fort out of pine needles while Terry would start walking home.

A golden rule for Terry was she had to go camping with us. She could leave when she wanted to, but she had to go first. It was family time. Of course she started walking home as soon as we got there. And, believe it or not, she walked the three miles home on a dirt road reading a Harlequin Romance novel. I guess "Scarlett" thought she was too good to bunk with us wretched farm hands.

Life ran in reverse at the lake. My dad did the cooking. I didn't have to fight over the bathroom, which turned out to be a makeshift outhouse. There was no bedtime, no grass to mow, and rarely did I have to brush my teeth. It was a place for rowing a boat, sinking a line, skipping a rock, lighting a fire, roasting a marshmallow, and catching fireflies. It was the way father Abraham lived.

Two camping trips were the hallmark of our family's experience in the wilderness: Loretta Lynn's Dude Ranch and Walt Disney Land.

Loretta Lynn's Dude Ranch had everything a kid could ask for: a creek, a pool, a magic show, and a Frostie Root Beer soda machine. The cans were so cold if you licked your hand the cans would stick to your flesh. For several summers this was our destination of choice. My dad even went to the trouble of building a camping trailer out of plywood to store our gear in trying to mimic an aluminum pop-up trailer. Loaded with a week of supplies, it put our little white van to the test. As a matter of fact, during our first attempt to climb the hill at the entrance to Loretta Lynn's, the clutch overheated and filled the interior with smoke. Everybody probably thought we were a bunch of hippies smoking weed. We actually didn't make it up the hill and had to get a little help from a ranch hand and a tractor. I wasn't embarrassed. I was just glad the Pringles didn't burn up.

While my dad started adjusting the clutch and my mother got busy setting things up for our week of fun, I'd put on what I would wear for the entire week- a pair of swim trunks. I'd run down to the creek and dive into the icy water where I lived for seven days. I got out of the water to roast hot dogs, eat Oreos, and drink Frostie Root Beer. It was a trial run of Heaven.

We really didn't do anything the whole week except catch a few camp shows at night. A guy named Ricky Rebel would sing a couple of songs and then a magician named Phooey Louie would saw someone in half or pull a rabbit out of his hat. I grew up raising rabbits and wasn't too impressed with the rabbit trick. I could put two rabbits in a cage and show you 200 a week later. I'd also seen my father saw off his own body parts and just tape them back on.

On the hill, along with the camp show, were the rich people with their fancy Airstream campers (all aluminum luxurious RV's built to last a lifetime) hooked up with electricity, running water and sewage. Literally their RV's were a little nicer than my house. Ok, I'm kidding...they were a lot nicer than my house. My dad, however, is a genius who can build anything. He built our house...by himself. Building a house requires several people, unless you're Timex. Imagine if one person had built the great pyramids, they might be a little less than perfect. So our house has imperfections, but it is unique and belongs in a museum.

The fact he had built a house gave him the courage to build his own Airstream. He went out and found a couple of old axels, took a welder and made a trailer. He then took a camper that fits in the bed of a truck and bolted it to the trailer. Then he took plywood and built a shell around it. To authenticate the Airstream look he painted it with silver roof paint. We took the invention to Florida.

We pulled the six thousand pound contraption with a 1972 green Dodge pickup with no air and an AM radio. I think we got about four miles per gallon while we drove 45mph for thirty hours to get to our first KOA stop in Tallahassee. My two sisters and I rode in the back of the truck all the way to Florida, blinded by the sun glaring off the silver roof paint of the camper in tow. We turned a few heads in 1983.

We did the whole Florida thing. We went to the beach, drank some salt water, and ate some sand. After almost drowning, we put a few seashells for souvenirs in a zip lock bag for later (should have never opened it when I got back). We drank some fresh orange juice at McDonald's and ate some fresh seafood at Long John Silvers. We went to Walt Disney Land and discovered Mickey Mouse can't talk.

We limped back home because the camper started having axel trouble and the truck started having engine trouble. The truck pulling the camper was the equivalent of a remote control car trying to pull a diesel truck (with the brakes on). The only thing worse than riding in the back of a truck across a hot Florida highway is riding in the back of a truck that is not moving. Like Apollo 13 we began to wonder if we would make it back home. This was the critical

43

moment. Would the homemade axel hold? Would the truck engine survive the intense heat of the July sun? Would the family dehydrate before re-entry? We made it back and celebrated by eating a steak and ravaging the salad bar at Western Sizzlin'.

A successful failure, you look at life and a lot of things don't work out as planned. But in those moments of challenge we forge some of our finest memories. A family who suffers together, stays together. We were tested and we all passed. We learned often what brings us comfort in the midst of discomfort is the trust we have in those around us. It is our decision whether we stay or leave, just like it was Terry's. If I were me again, I'd climb back into that truck and do it again, not only because in some weird way it was fun but also because in some weird way it was fundamental to my story.

Our family time was called a successful failure in that we returned home but never perfected the art of traveling around the country in our homemade Airstream. In the following years I have determined our limited resources prevented us from achieving our goal of becoming professionals. It was beyond our control and impacted most of my childhood, in a positive fashion. As for me, these early years of camping were not my last. I have continued to confront the elements and assume the challenges nature presents. I sometimes catch myself staring into a campfire and remembering my changes of fortune on our family trips, thinking about the parents who worked so hard to take me there. I look at the fire and wonder, will I continue to come back? And who will I bring with me?

"Ebenezer Scrooge: But you were always a good man of business Jacob. The Ghost of Jacob Marley: Mankind should be our business, Ebenezer, but we seldom attend to it... as you shall see."

...from the movie The Scrooge

THE DEVIL DRIVES
A SALT TRUCK

I can't really talk about growing up without talking about snow days. These small miracles were God's way of saving me from the monotony of math and his way of punishing my mother for hiding Oreos in the freezer. For me, snow days were a welcomed reprieve from sitting still, sitting up straight, and breathing chalk dust. For my mother they were a dreaded refresher course on what it felt like to be a monkey trying to survive a plunge into a river of piranhas. And for my father, snow days were a seasonal sacrament that reconnected his heart with his spirit of survival.

Snow days resulted from two types of precipitation: snow or ice. While snow presented its own set of problems, ice had the power to paralyze a town. And that is exactly what happened in 1976.

When I was six years old a major ice storm shut down our school system for five days when falling trees cut power throughout the county. Iced in, we spent the daylight hours sliding down hills and watching icicles grow. Without power, we spent the nighttime in the dark, huddled around our fireplace reminiscing about noodles and barbequed rabbit. After four days without power, our hunger got the best of us and my mother set about cooking a pot of chili in the fireplace. Starving, we patiently watched my mother stir the steaming chili for four hours while we munched on crackers in anticipation of the feast to follow. At the precise moment the chili was almost finished there was a sudden shift in the logs and my mother's attempt at saving it sent a ball of soot and ash flying into our dinner. It felt like I was watching my dog get run over. Indeed the ash was fatal. We threw it out and snacked on potted meat and pickles. I think I remember crying about it.

Seeing how difficult is was to cook in a fireplace, Timex eventually invested in a woodstove to ensure his family would stay warm and not go hungry. His memories of frost on the rafters during his own childhood motivated him to often run the wood stove wide open achieving an ambient temperature of ninety. Sometimes my sisters couldn't sit in the den because it melted their makeup. Now that he is older, Timex enjoys keeping it hot enough to melt the M&Ms in the candy dish but cool enough to avoid my mother's fuzzy housecoat spontaneously combusting. It does smoke at times.

Although unlikely, I would love to see my parents retire to Florida, buy a wonderful condo on the beach, look around, and hear my father ask, *"Where's the wood stove? Quarter of million and no wood stove?"* I guarantee my dad could learn how to burn palm trees and clams in a woodstove. He's a genius.

Timex believes the art of surviving in the winter involves staying warm and having a plentiful supply of pecans to shell. Shelling a pecan is like cracking a safe to get a penny. Timex likes pennies. He has a light in his eyes when winter intrudes and he sits in his living room, fire roaring, socks steaming, shells flying, and Paul Harvey talking. He looks like a famished but happy Santa.

When I was a child, Timex prepared for our winter survival by cutting enough firewood to heat the White House and loading the 1972 green Dodge with cinder blocks for traction. The woodcutting consumed my Saturdays for about two months in the fall. I didn't mind being serenaded by a chainsaw and anointed with sawdust because I wanted to be a lumberjack. But before I could throw a hatchet into a tree I had to learn to split firewood with an axe.

I broke a dozen wooden handles learning how to chop wood when eventually Timex got tired of my miscues and welded a metal handle to my axe head. After that, a miscue was like hitting an iron pole with an aluminum baseball bat. At first it felt like I was getting electrocuted and then it felt like someone was sticking needles between my fingers. As numbness ensued, a high pitch ring developed in my ears while my eyes vibrated in their socket. It was a great motivator to learn to hit my darn target.

Sometimes the way a father affirms his son is by trusting him to do something dangerous but important. At the time it felt like I was in charge of the fort and there were about a million Indians. When he handed me that metal axe handle it was as if he was saying, "*Son,*

I'll be gone for a long time and it's going to be a hard winter. I may not make it back in time but I know it will be ok because I am leaving you here." We never ran out of wood in the winter and now I can slice a tomato with an axe.

While my father showed his love by giving me an axe with a metal handle, God showed his love to me by giving me a long hard winter. My favorite thing to do in the winter was eat supper. My second favorite thing to do was watch the weather forecast for hints of impending icy doom. All I needed was a ten percent chance of snow within a one hundred mile radius and immediately I would start selling the idea of the storm of the century to my family, friends, and anybody who would listen. With the Bible verse, *"With faith the size of a mustard seed, you can move a mountain,"* I tried to catapult the small chance forward by begging God on my knees and promising I would serve in his Kingdom. I had no idea He would hold me to it.

With snow in the forecast it was difficult to fall asleep. It felt like Christmas Eve, like I was waiting on Santa to come and leave me presents. I wrestled all through the night, in part because my mother made me wear a t-shirt, which I hated, and in part because I was expecting a miracle. My dreams took me inside snow globes to find myself pleasantly trapped and munching on a gingerbread house. My nightmares took me inside greenhouses where I prayed with Frosty the Snowman as he melted in my arms. Shortly after I would wake up wet, sweating in that stupid T-shirt!

Early the next morning, tired from my dreams and wet from my nightmares, I would crawl out of my bed, wipe my eyes, and rub the condensation off the windows to squint and see a world of white. There, peering through my portal, I would sometimes cry because I believed God was listening.

The next thirty minutes were spent with my two sisters huddled not around the fireplace but rather around the radio. We were simply waiting to hear, *"Madison County schools will be closed today."* Those seven words sounded like Holy Scripture to me and I was aware they were God- breathed. After a few victory laps around the house, we were busy layering up with clothes and pairs of rubber boots. I dashed outside as if I was running to meet my bride on my wedding day.

Outside, I was greeted by a completely new landscape. One good thing about snow was it covered all the junk in our yard and made even the most dilapidated shed fit for a fairy tale. I always believed if tax assessments were done on snow days, no one could afford the payment. It was simply the best the world will ever look and the best I thought God could do. Yet with all there was to see, my fondest memory of a snow day was the silence. I think the silence magnified the beauty much like a deaf person has a better sense of sight. The absence of sound helped me listen to my spirit. It renewed me and reminded me there was a heaven and a God who loved children.

The mornings were spent sledding, building snowmen, and constructing forts. The occasional sting of a random snowball to the face would interrupt an otherwise perfect time that ended with hot stew and a glowing red woodstove. It was after lunch when all #$%! would break loose.

Just as we would be preparing for another round of throwing snowballs, the faint sound of the salt truck would freeze us in place with the look of horror on our face. It reminded me of an old movie where the children are at play and the air raid sirens go off warning warplanes are approaching and everyone screams and runs for the bomb shelter. With tears in our eyes, we simply watched the county truck drive toward us and throw salt on God's perfection. I was never brave enough to look, but I am certain the driver had horns and a red tail. The devil drove a salt truck. There were enough of us that we could have ambushed the truck and set it on fire but that would have just aided in the melting of snow. If the county was really concerned about the safety of kids they would have sent an ice cream truck with a really loud bell.

These snow days, these answers to my prayers, these silent white miracles, were the highlight of my childhood. They brought my family together, simplified our lives, and huddled us around a woodstove. Without electricity neighbors checked on neighbors, workers stayed home, and conversations and memories came out of the dark. Impending doom turned out to be a blessing.

One obstacle I face is that I am in such a hurry. When it snows I am busy at the coffee shop rather than spending time around the fire eating potted meat and pickles. My life is filled to the brim with

50

business, cleaning, and yard maintenance. My house is beautiful and my life is full but my heart is empty. I sit in important meetings craving stimulating conversation. I sit stoic in church dying for laughter and joy. I sit at home with the TV on and the radio playing but I sit in silence. My knowledge of real, meaningful conversation is fading into the future. Now I text instead of talk, email instead of entertain, and drive thru instead of sit down. If I am lucky a cold icy disaster will descend upon me and rescue me from my busy life. If I am brave I'll attack the salt trucks. If I am smart I won't use fire.

The Chicken Whisperer lived a very simplified life and dedicated his time to people. He believed God would meet his needs. He wasn't lazy; he just funneled his energy toward loving people rather than accumulating stuff. He said it is a sad thing when people spend their whole life collecting things for their grandchildren to sell at yard sales. At one point in his life he told a friend of his to stop what he had been doing all his life and do something totally different. His love was so powerful, his friend did it, and, as you will find out a little later this is why I am who I am. I am who I am because somebody stopped what they were doing and did something totally different.

"I have learned never leave your partner-especially in a fire.
... from the movie Fireproof

TEACH ME TO BURN

I must confess there is a sincere desire in me to watch things burn, and roast (especially chicken). It feels good to say that. It feels good to be honest. I don't enjoy watching people get hurt or losing property, I'm just memorized by the rhythm of flames. A lot of people are. In a city where there are life saving surgeries being performed; where the cornerstones of the community are being buried; and where at any given moment a hundred important people are doing a hundred important things; everybody would rather follow a fire truck.

Even the human story begins with God hanging a big ball of fire in the sky and calling it day. And according to Exodus, not long after we arrived this "day" rained down on our heads accompanied by a little brimstone. Ironically, God also used fire constructively when He made a bush talk and when He led a confused nation to the Promised Land. Fire it seems is woven throughout the fabric of our heritage from Sodom to Chicago. And in childhood it was my security blanket.

Who can blame a child for wanting to play with matches? Our ancestors devoted themselves to the very task of finding a way to bring fire into the home, first to keep warm, and then to light torches and candles so we could continue to shell purple hull peas past sunset. But it didn't take them long to learn that fire is an incredible resource with an incredible liability. They fought to keep it from burning their homes, their schools, and their farms. They built fire stations, fire extinguishers, fire alarms, and told their kids don't play with matches but then turned around and put candles on their birthday cake. This was like celebrating an alcoholic's sobriety with a six-pack. Personally, I could have cared less about making a wish on my birthday, I just wanted to watch the candles burn.

When my family went on those camping trips, like the Israelites, a fire followed us. The last, but best, thing we always did in setting up camp was we built a fire. We even built one if we were camping in July for the simple reason that mosquitoes don't like smoked human flesh.

I learned to properly sit around a campfire I didn't need a chair, I just needed a long stick. A stick around a fire was the equivalent of a pole while fishing: you just got to have one. These sticks kept me entertained for hours as I poked the fire, threatened my sisters with the burning ends, and made neon circles with the red tips in the dark. I tried to do other things with them like roast marshmallows but even these succumbed to becoming mini torches setting the stage for a tiny version of a medieval war. Try getting a flaming marshmallow off your chest!

As I grew older, I had less supervision and began to unwisely experiment with throwing various items into the fire to see what would happen: plastic bottles, whole cans of soda, cheese whip, and empty cans of bug repellant. Interestingly the can of cheese whip

53

gave me the best boom, I just had to watch out for hot cheese landing on my head.

Eventually I learned I had to respect the things I love, including fire. My first brush with death by fire came the night my parents put my oldest sister in charge of the house while they went out to dinner. Terry decided to cook popcorn and started heating some oil on the stove (pre microwave days) and then joined us in the living room to watch *Love Boat*. A few minutes later we saw the shadow of flames dancing on the walls followed by an encore of thick black smoke. All three of us rushed into the kitchen to see our popcorn pan turned into a fire-breathing dragon. With a lid it was easily slain but its friends, "black pot" and "black ceiling," were alive and well. Crying, Terry took an S.O.S pad and started scrubbing the blackened pot but there was no hope for cleaning the ceiling. She had failed my parents and she had failed me: no popcorn. I had told her I wanted cinnamon toast anyway.

The following summer another brush with death by fire occurred when a forest fire threatened our home. I knew it was serious when we started seeing city fire trucks go by our house in the country. My mother was alarmed enough to start getting things together for a possible evacuation. She asked us to go grab a few things to keep us company in case we were gone for a couple of days, things like shoes and extra clothes. I was thinking we might come back to a pile of ashes so I grabbed a security blanket and my father's ceramic dog full of pennies.

My respect deepened the Monday my father came home with a few serious burns after fighting a house fire. Just a few days later, we returned from shopping for school clothes and my mother was broiling burgers in the oven for dinner when the smoke alarm started going off. Fearful of a popcorn repeat, or ending up like my father, I rushed to the kitchen to investigate and saw flames leap out toward my mother's face when she opened the oven door. Scared, I bolted to the living room, grabbed my new pair of jeans still in the Sears bag, and ran past all my precious family. In my defense, that was the only new jeans I would get that Fall. I was punished by the screen door, which was locked and almost broke my wrist when I tried to stiff-arm it going 20 mph.

All of this love for its potential and respect for its power was the recipe for a legendary romance with fireworks. Nothing fascinates a kid more than the combination of high risks, loud noises, colorful sparks, and intense smoke (this is why David Letterman has a cute girl with a metal dress and a grinder on his show).

Unfortunately my romance was on a budget and I usually spent the Fourth of July trying to catch the parachutes of the fireworks the neighbors had shot off. The next morning we would scavenge the yard looking for remnants of unexploded bottle rockets. If we were real lucky we found a partially used roman candle. This was like finding the Ark of the Covenant with a metal detector, or like being really hungry and finding a three piece chicken dinner with potatoes, gravy, slaw, and an extra biscuit. My dream has always been to be in a hot air balloon in the middle of New York' City's Fourth of July fireworks display. Dumb dream. Balloon flammable.

55

I even wanted fireworks for Christmas. I would have worn gunpowder cologne. I would have slept with a gross of bottle rockets if my mother had let me. Every time I saw something that said made in China I thought, *"Wow! These are the same people who invented fireworks!"*

Although they were dangerous, I was soothed by the wonderment of things burning and popping. Some kids need a pacifier, some suck their thumb, but I just needed a book of matches, a stick, and some gunpowder. I was a kid who liked to take chances and I was also a kid who occasionally got burned.

I once heard if you set yourself on fire the world will come to see you burn. The Chicken Whisperer said this was a good idea. He believed when we love people we become light in darkness, and because so many people live in the absence of love, which is darkness, we should shine. He often spoke of living life in terms of shining. He believed people were blind by choice because they were afraid to approach light, afraid to be loved, because it would reveal their deficiencies. This means prideful people choose to remain in darkness, freeze to death, and suffer because of the shame of their hidden deficiencies. He said what people fail to realize is that light (love) is a great equalizer. Our fear of being ashamed of our deficiencies is neutralized by the common denominator of the fact we are all deficient. And better yet, although true love does indeed often reveal these deficiencies, it also often overwhelms them with grace, so rather than shame we experience relief. He said because this type of grace-filled love actually frees people and keeps them from freezing, we should set ourselves on fire and shine.

While trying to stay focused on the things that matter, my inspiration for living, loving, and burning sometimes comes from a conversation between a cockroach and a fire-obsessed moth hanging on my bathroom wall. It says:

i was talking to a moth
the other evening
he was trying to break into
an electric light bulb
and fry himself on the wires

why do you fellows
pull this stunt i asked him
because it is the conventional
thing for moths or why
if that had been an uncovered
candle instead of an electric
light bulb you would
now be a small unsightly cinder
have you no sense

plenty of it he answered
but at times we get tired
of using it
we get bored with the routine
and crave beauty
and excitement

fire is beautiful
and we know that if we get
too close it will kill us
but what does that matter
it is better to be happy
for a moment
and be burned up with beauty
than to live a long time

and be bored all the while

so we wad all our life up
into one little roll
and then we shoot the roll
that is what life is for
it is better to be a part of beauty
for one instant and then cease to
exist than to exist forever
and never be a part of beauty

our attitude toward life
is come easy go easy
we are like human beings
used to be before they became
too civilized to enjoy themselves

and before i could argue him
out of his philosophy
he went and immolated himself
on a patent cigar lighter

i do not agree with him
myself i would rather have
half the happiness and twice
the longevity
but at the same time i wish
there was something i wanted
as badly as he wanted to fry himself

by: Don Marquis

Someone once said if we find something worth dying for we'll find something worth living for. So much of our passion for life, for love, for everything, withers like a limb broken in the storm somewhere along the way. Now we find ourselves consumed with career moves, mortgage payments, and painting houses when probably what we need to do is catch a few fireflies, roast a marshmallow, or cast ourselves into someone else's beauty. We fear being foolish. We are a fool because we fear.

Willy Wonka: "Charlie, don't forget what happened to the man who suddenly got everything he always wanted." Charlie: "What happened?" Willy Wonka: "He lived happily ever after
...from the movie Willy Wonka and the Chocolate Factory

CANDY CIGARETTES

I f your child were thirsty would you give him gasoline? If your child were hungry would you give him an oil filter? Then why did my parents feed me licorice? And what about those black jellybeans on Easter? Everything is going great- strawberry, lips licked; lime, tongue dancing; orange, saliva building; grape, eyes watering; and then BAM, an oil filter!

Even my Christmas stocking was not exempt from the intrusion of nasty. I'd run to the fireplace with visions of gumdrops in my head, grab my stuffed stocking, and pour the treasure out on the floor to reveal pounds of delight infiltrated by a roll of Necco Wafers. Necco Wafers tasted like deodorant with a touch of hairspray. Finding those horrible pastel discs in my stocking was like finding a hair, no a ponytail, in my meatloaf.

But the king of nasty was a horehound, the brown version of the lemon drop, brown because it was made with cat poop. Whoever came up with the idea of hardening cough syrup and rolling it around in raw sugar committed a crime against childhood. If Congress wanted to change the world, they should have put that guy behind bars.

The seventies and eighties however birthed some all time greats like candy cigarettes and Big League Chew. There was nothing like

59

riding a bike with a box of candy cigs rolled up in your t-shirt sleeve. You were the king of cool. The only thing that could make you cooler was riding one handed and stuffing half a pack of grape Big League Chew in your jaw while purple spit dripped on your handlebars. Whoever came up with the idea of mimicking tobacco with candy should be given a gold star, and a scolding from his mother.

Christmas was by far my favorite holiday but running a close second was its arch nemesis, Halloween. There were hayrides, bonfires, carved pumpkins, cool costumes, and tons of free candy. What a great idea: one night a year you dress up like a monster, take a paper bag, ring a doorbell, and the people you bother give you candy because they would rather treat than be tricked. And not once in all my years of trick or treating did I ever get one single piece of licorice, Necco wafers, or Horehounds. Nope, only my parents pushed their childhood memories of the Great Depression on me. Of course my mother also kept ginger snaps in the cookie jar while she hid Oreos in the freezer. No, the nice adults in the neighborhood always gave me good candy. I figured out how to tell who went to church: cheap heathens gave out tiny Dum Dums but Christians gave out big Blowpops. Only the devil himself would have given out licorice, Horehounds, or Necco Wafers.

This childhood experience has motivated me as an adult to be conscientious about what I give kids at Halloween. I prefer to hand out two liter cokes, regular size candy bars, and fireworks. When I get rich I'm going to have a Hibachi grill to cook S'mores; hot

60

chocolate made with steamed milk; and cartons of candy cigarettes with real lighters.

Even nature has its own occasional nuisance in the production of sugar. Honey, for example, is made from the nectar of flowers by an insect with a stinger. Bees repeatedly regurgitate spit and then fan the goo with their little angel wings to reduce water content so it won't ferment. Why can't wasps be this productive, like make lifesavers or something? Why can't spiders weave little socks for babies or silk scarves for grandmothers? Bees on the other hand are making the world a better place until you step on one and then all &#$@! breaks loose! It's funny that when my foot was swollen the size of a watermelon and smelling like vinegar, I never once thought about being thankful for Honey Buns. I was a shallow kid.

It was against this backdrop of honey guarded by bees, stockings tainted with Necco Wafers, and Easter baskets corrupted with black jellybeans that I began to understand the world is just as dangerous as it is exciting. I was learning that we live among the remnants of a paradise lost and the sacraments are clues that once upon a time really existed. I was learning that as we walk among the wreckage we encounter the imposters and the posers like licorice and horehounds, and through trial and tribulation we find there is an incredible difference between heaven's honey and artificial flavoring. I was learning how to respect an incredible plan of redemption that does not hide, but rather hangs the apple in front of us, a love that gives us a choice and a chance to taste both so we never wonder if something good is being withheld. The curse of contrast turns out to be a blessing after all because unless I had tasted darkness, I would not have known my need for Light.

"The world is full of nice, ordinary little people who live in nice, ordinary little houses on the ground. But didn't you ever dream of a house up on a tree top?"   *...from the movie Swiss Family Robinson*

THORN TREE TREEHOUSE

G rowing up on a farm I was surrounded by men of ingenuity; men who believed JB Weld and duct tape could repair the space shuttle; men who could take apart a toaster and use the parts to make two toasters. It was only natural I would follow in their footsteps and become a co-creator.

Before I created anything I had to get acquainted with my resources. Basically this is where I took inventory of what my Dad and Grandfather had in their tool sheds and planned a raid. This is also where I first tested the theory that forgiveness is easier to get than permission.

Deciding what *was* and what *wasn't* available for construction projects involved a learning curve. When my dad let me use a chainsaw at the age of ten I assumed I had access to all power tools but learned the hard way (after I left them out in the rain) power tools belong to the one who pays for them. I also found out that really long thick boards stacked neatly in a pile belonged to a set of scaffolding, after I used them to build a shoe rack, a really nice thick shoe rack.

An even bigger challenge than learning what I could or couldn't use was learning how to put my projects together with inadequate fasteners. I realized the Egyptians didn't use anything, but once you put a ten- ton rock somewhere it isn't going to move. I tried bent rusty nails and screws but eventually found an abundant supply of bailing twine. I never learned to tie a knot until I was twelve so my creations ceased to exist shortly after they were crafted. My knot tying was delayed because rather than attending Boy Scouts, I had to follow my mother and sisters to Girl Scouts. But luckily, I learned to sell cookies.

Regardless of what held my construction projects together, they could be divided into two categories: big and dangerous. And sometimes the categories collided.

The biggest project was when Jim, a childhood friend, and I decided we needed a log cabin. It looked easy enough, plus we both had plenty of practice playing with Lincoln logs. So with a sharp axe in hand we jumped on our bicycles and headed for the lake, the perfect place for our ponderosa.

We started looking nearby for tall straight pines and found a nice group of them fairly close. Eight hours later we had chopped down about twelve trees and were really starting to feel like burly lumberjacks yelling "TIMBER!" but we both realized we had forgotten to wear flannel shirts.

Back home, still without any adults aware that we were chopping down the forest, we pulled out the encyclopedia and read up on primitive log cabin construction and pretty much concluded we would be as comfy as Thoreau on Walden's Pond in just a couple of weeks.

The next weekend we returned with a sap covered axe and blistered covered hands to survey our fallen pile of wealth. With tears in our eyes, we stared at the fifty branches on each log that would have to be chopped off one by one. Our cabin's square footage was immediately reduced by seventy-five percent. After a few weekends of branch cutting we then tackled the daunting task of peeling off the bark with a hatchet. This turned out to be as hard as trying to filet a live fish in water. We decided to stack the logs and let the bark rot off. We were moving on to fireplace construction.

The obvious obstacle was where to get a thousand bricks, but I had a plan. About a tenth of a mile away from our construction site was an old well lined with bricks. So with a shovel and a wagon we started excavation. After about two weeks of digging and pulling a wagon full of bricks a tenth of a mile we decided our fireplace would be more like a small barbecue grill. We needed a mule, but all we had was a Cheerio breakfast and a gallon of lime Kool-aid.

Eventually we managed to get a pole barn frame up with a piece of tin covering a tiny part of the roof. It looked like a relic from the gold rush although it was only four weeks old. Not only were the Indians here first, they were also smart enough to just use tents. Our fort idea also fell through when the adults noticed the skyline changing and didn't believe our beaver infestation story. Beavers don't build barbeque grills.

The most difficult and dangerous undertaking we ever assumed was our decision to build a clubhouse in a thorn tree. This was the equivalent of putting piranhas in your swimming pool. It was a challenge that gained us a little notoriety in the neighborhood.

Why we chose a tree with four-inch thorns was simply a matter of its beautiful branch arrangement. From a distance it looked friendly enough and we were committed to building our castle in the tree before we stumbled upon the fact it was cursed with thorns. It was sort of like seeing a pretty girl and then discovering she laughs like a seal: you kiss her anyway. Plus, we decided the thorns would help keep intruders away and come in mighty handy as toothpicks when we were eating beef jerky.

Again the project was never completed. When we had assembled enough room for the two of us to sit and have lunch (beef jerky and beanie weenies) adults condemned the project and we were forced to abandon our palace. The Wright Brothers always left town for Kittyhawk to do their experimenting and now I know why. I miss sitting in thorns, eating Slim Jims, and watching the sunset.

As a child I got in the habit of starting but not finishing. In reflection it was often because of a third party's opinion, someone who looked at my dreams from a perspective of safety. But I am one of the few people in the world who has ever ridden a bicycle with an axe or used a thorn as a toothpick. Although I wasn't gaining a reputation as a competent contractor I was signaling to society I was going to live outside the box.

Now I know that permission is easier to get than forgiveness simply because most people can't forgive. I know the real tools we need in life are forged in the heart not in a furnace. And last but not least, I know that all things we craft with our hands turn to dust: log cabins, tree houses, coliseums, and even pyramids.

My construction projects simply enabled me to spend time with friends. Like so many things in life, the means often justified the fact that there was no end. I've learned the only monument to our life, the only record that we were here, might be these near death experiences we encounter, the risks we take with friends, and the laughter and tears that often erupt on the journey. All of our legacies should first include love, and anything that's left should be devoted to laughter.

A lot of our identities are sadly attached to the house we live in. If we were asked to trade houses with someone in a lower income bracket what would happen to our lives. The only way a house can have a positive or negative impact on our life is if we have a corrupt value system. True identity cannot burn down.

The Chicken Whisperer believed the poor were blessed in a way, and the rich were cursed in a way. He had both types of friends, and each had their own challenges. Yet I cannot remember ever reading anything about the Chicken Whisperer's house. His mother gave birth to him in a barn and his father had a mansion with many rooms. But as for him, he said the only place he ever wanted to live was inside of the hearts of the people he loved.

"I have no idea to this day what those two Italian ladies were singing about. Truth is, I don't want to know. Some things are better left unsaid. I'd like to think they were singing about something so beautiful, it can't be expressed in words, and it makes your heart ache because of it. I tell you, those voices soared higher and farther than anybody in a grey place dares to dream. It was as if some beautiful bird had flapped into our drab little cage and made these walls dissolve away, and for the briefest of moments, every last man in Shawshank felt free."

...from the movie Shawshank Redemption

THE SOUND OF MUSIC

I grew up with a lot of sweet sounds in my life: bacon frying, window units, Paul Harvey, crop dusters, fireworks, school bells, oven timers, power tools, attic fans, and country music.

Today the multi-talented, naturally beautiful, and totally transparent Taylor Swift rules the radio and directs the dreams of young men (I have both her Cds), but in 1980 it was a woman named Dolly.

Dolly Parton grew up in a dirt-poor town called Locust Ridge nestled in the hills of the Smokey Mountains. She was one of twelve siblings who lived in a rustic one-room cabin. She met her husband, Carl, at the Wishy Washy in downtown Nashville at the age of twenty while pursuing her music career. His first words to her were, *"You're going to get sunburned out there little lady."* My first words to Taylor Swift would be, *"Age is just a number."*

The first song I remember hearing Dolly sing on the radio was "I Will Always Love You." I heard it on a portable transistor radio swinging as high as possible with a grape Popsicle dripping down

68

my bare chest. I don't recall exactly what had upset me, but I was feeling lonely. I was trying to fight back the tears but ended up letting them go, making sure my sisters didn't see me turning into a puddle. It was as if God put on a blonde wig and sang me a song. That song was like a tender kiss, and thus my love affair with country music was underway.

My favorite childhood memories come with a soundtrack of country music, a soundtrack created via AM radio, occasional vinyl 45s, and low quality speakers. But in spite of the fact it flew to me on broken wings, it was always strong enough to lift my spirits. Eddie Arnold's "Make the World Go Away" has never sounded better than it did while riding in a green Dodge pickup truck with a chainsaw under my feet on the way to cut firewood with my father on a fall Saturday morning. I miss hearing Tanya Tucker's "Delta Dawn" crackling through an antique radio on hot, humid summer nights while lying on my back watching fireflies with the taste of strawberries still on my lips. And I still dream of those magical spring campfires where Jimmy Dean's story of "*Big Bad John*" came to life on a portable hand held transistor radio when the smoke gave me an excuse to cry. Even though I now listen to all of these songs in high quality on my iPhone, I wish I could push a distort, crackle button to make it sound like they were singing in a cereal box again.

What I loved then is what I love now: the story telling of country music. A good song is like a mini-movie for those of us with attention deficit. Depending on when and where I first heard a song, determined how it changed my life.

Inspired by the song "Convoy" there was a time in my life when I wanted to be a truck driver hauling logs and hogs, running from "Bears" and "Smokies." Thanks to the song "Patches" I believed I too would lose my father to fever, take over the farm, but stay in school because it was *"Daddy's strictest rule."* "The Coward of the County" got me ready to fight for my girl even if my dad was giving me bad advice from prison. And "Teddy Bear" inspired me to search on my hand me down CB for crippled, fatherless children who needed money and a ride in a truck. I lived my life under the influence, not of drugs or alcohol, but the influence of good music.

Country music taught me about love. "The Rose" taught me love is a river and a razor, a hunger and a need, a dance and a dream, and a flower and seed. "Ring of Fire" taught me love is a burning thing that makes a fiery ring, and eventually I would fall into this fire, and the flames would go higher and higher. "The End of the World" taught me when I fell under its spell, the world would go right on turning, even though my heart was burning. And "I Wouldn't Have Missed It for the World" taught me love comes and goes like the wind and all good things must end, but just to see her smile would make it worth my while.

It would be years later in college before I went to my first country music concert. My friend Bill dragged me to a post prime John Conlee show at the Oklahoma State Fairgrounds. John showed up about three hours late, which gave the three hundred people waiting nothing to do but drink. One of these three hundred people decided it would be fun to roll down three sections of concrete stairs and had to be carried out in an ambulance (the guy almost made me spill my

70

hot chocolate). Once the concert started I sat and watched about ten forty-year-old women climb an eight-foot chain link fence to get to a pair of rose-colored glasses John was wearing. He sat there and sang the whole song watching them trying to get to the top. It reminded me a lot of Saturday morning wrestling.

Every music genre has it's own unique set of fans. But country music has children, and I was one of them. Like a mother, it sang me to sleep, taught me about love, and mended my wounds. Like a father, it showed me how to do things, pushed me to try hard, and made me believe in myself. And like a grandfather, it helped me laugh, inspired me to dream, and when it was time, showed me the healing power of tears.

I have come to believe all of our lives are set to music, and sometimes, when we listen, we can hear it; and sometimes yet, when we are blessed, we get to share this music with the world. The Chicken Whisperer often spoke of our life having an imbedded theme, a destiny, a path to God. He said that this theme involves the complete pursuit of two things: loving God and loving our neighbor. Once we hear it, we are ready to receive God's love and love Him in return. Once we are ready to share it, we are ready to love others.

"Either we do not know what part of ourselves to give, or, more often than not, the part we have to give is not wanted. So it is those who we live with and love and should know that elude us. But we can still reach out to them, we can love completely without complete understanding."

...from the movie A River Runs Through It

BASS FISHING BAPTISM

There are three paths to manhood- chest hair, a bloody nose, and a big fish. Sometimes they happen in reverse order, and if you're really lucky they all happen at the same time.

Learning to fish was a sacred event in my life. It has almost changed me as much as my baptism. Every kid in the world should learn to do something their ancestors had to do to survive. They need to have an experience in their life that says, "I man. Man strong." Fishing was my invitation into the human race.

I began my fishing career with a rustic, but efficient, eight-foot cane pole and a three-inch red and white bobber. With no money, I had to use a poor man's bait---a can of worms I dug up around the calf barn. Just like anything sacred, fishing requires a sacrifice, and for the most part the worms cooperated, or at least they kept their mouths shut. I liked this primitive form of bait because it made me feel like Huckleberry Finn, who reminded me of Mark Twain, who reminded me of Colonel Sanders, who reminded me of fried chicken. I like fried chicken. When I caught a fish with a worm it made me feel like Captain Ahab harpooning Moby Dick, which made me feel like Rambo spearing a squirrel, which made me feel like a caveman spearing a pterodactyl (a giant flying bird). I like fried chicken. When I caught my first fish I knew I was hooked.

After yanking fish out of the water with a cane pole for a couple of years, I graduated to a Zebco 404, which is barely one step above a Snoopy reel. (If you're serious about catching fish never use a Snoopy reel, or a Little Mermaid reel). Fishing with a Snoopy reel is like handing a banana to a hungry gorilla and then trying to take it back.

Eventually I perfected the art of casting and got bold enough to throw off the training wheels and go after bottom dwelling catfish. To fish for catfish you have to be prepared to put &*#! on a hook, stare at a pole for thirty minutes, and withstand a heartbeat of 200. Nothing compares to catching catfish, except eating them with vinegar slaw and hush puppies. And don't forget the ketchup.

Everybody should buy at least one bag of stink bait even if you don't fish. The smell of stink bait will make you pray to be sprayed by a skunk. It will make you appreciate a bath in sewage. You will do anything to get the stench of stink bait out of your nostrils and off your hands. Why anything would want to eat stink bait is a tougher question than "where do dead pets go?" I think they might use them to make stink bait.

However, the best way to catch catfish doesn't even involve a pole, it involves a milk jug. There is no greater thrill, no greater risk, and no greater reward than jug fishing. The giant that would snap the typical line on a fishing pole can be caught with the properly rigged jug. Just have a plan to handle him when you get him in the boat. A small revolver will usually do the trick. Just don't shoot a hole in your boat.

You jug fish by taking your household empty milk jugs and attaching short pieces of nylon string and strong hooks. You then wait until dark; get in a boat and bait the hooks; place them randomly in the pond; and then row back to shore. You then sit on the pond bank by a fire with a high-powered flashlight, and when you see a jug take off across the water like Jaws, you jump in and chase it down in the boat. If you ever see the jug go completely under, prepare yourself for a fish the size of a hot water heater.

I used to escape to the lake as often as possible with my Zebco 33 and my dad's tackle box. Sometimes I took my bike and sometimes I just walked the three miles. The day I hooked Nessy I rode my bike.

Believe it or not, I caught Nessy in January during a winter thaw. Nessy was nine pounds of large mouth bass (I have the picture to prove it). I named her Nessy after her smaller cousin the Loch Ness Monster.

It was about 60 degrees and I was dressed in high- water jeans and a thin camo T-shirt. My hair was so thick it was sometimes referred to as "Eagle's Nest." I looked weird, but it was to my advantage.

After about fifty casts I realized I was wasting my time so I decided to call it quits and started reeling in my lure to head to the house. I was about to yank it out of the water when it was ten feet from the shore but suddenly I saw a huge swirl erupt close to the bank. A second later I felt the strike. It was as if I had just hooked an underwater nuclear submarine. Luckily, I had my drag set for Crappie and my reel responded with whining while releasing string rather than my line snapping in two.

I wish I could tell you my reel started smoking and I battled the behemoth for two hours but the truth is... she gave up. I think she got a glimpse of me from the water and thought, "*Dang, this kid looks funny. He needs a little boost. I'll be his trophy.*" I simply pulled her to shore in about ten seconds, reached down, grabbed her by her mouth, and, in the excitement, threw her over my head to ensure she would not flop back into the water. I turned around and she was gone, nowhere to be found. At first I thought it was all a hallucination from eating too much left over fermented fruitcake, but then I spotted my beautiful Nessy hanging in the tree like a Christmas ornament.

I got her out of the tree, tied her to my bike, and rode home like Paul Revere warning the settlers the British were coming. It was a wonderful celebration, and a decent supper. I couldn't afford to get her mounted. My memory and proof of Nessy is a simple three by five photograph of the girl who made me feel like a man. She changed my life.

Fishing was, and still is, a powerful metaphor in my life when it comes to relationships. Relationships and fishing both depend on tying the right kind of knot and you're wasting your time if you don't. They both involve getting your hands dirty. You can't be afraid to get messy if you want a Nessy or if you want to let someone else into your heart. Relationships and fishing are about connecting two different species, be willing to learn something you don't know. All good fishermen learn how to swim and all good husbands learn how to cook. Relationships and fishing can both lead to a kiss when you get a really nice one. Don't be afraid to celebrate, even when no one is watching. They are both full of surprises. Be prepared to catch a turtle, a snake, and eventually a trophy.

By the way, I practice catch and release, and I wish I could say it is because I am environmentally aware, but the truth is I hate cleaning fish. If I want clean fish I can go to a sushi bar.

"My 9th grade science teacher once told me that if you put a frog in boiling water, it'll jump out, but if you put it in cold water and heat it up gradually, it'll just sit there and slowly boil to death." "What's that, Harry, your recipe for frog soup?" "That's my recipe for disaster."

...from the movie Dante's Peak

SURVIVING MT. SAINT HELENS

I had three fears in adolescence—bathrooms, rejection, and Eddie.

An elementary school bathroom was like a preview to Dante's Inferno. When I swung a stall door open at noon (I was lucky if there was a door) I might be staring at something that happened before class ever started. Flushing was something kids did once the toilet was full, thus creating a Niagara Falls effect. There were always puddles of pee around the urinals and fingerprints all over the mirrors. But the soap dispenser was always full? Yet nothing reminded me of Satan himself more than the stench of hot steaming urine.

For some reason I'll never understand, (one of those questions I'll ask when I get to heaven) a few guys peed on the bathroom radiators trying to mark their territory. The stench of the steam made me puke and motivated me to train my bladder to hold three gallons of urine because I couldn't bear to go to the "bathfume." I peed once a week. It took thirty minutes and six flushes.

Needless to say, when I walked into my current house and found these huge radiators in almost every room I started trying to rip the adornments of hell out of my house and take them to the landfill. Unfortunately, I discovered they weighed a little more than a small planet and I was stuck with them. I found I still held my breath when I looked at one. My bladder also reverted back to previous training, but because I'm older, I now have to pee twice a week.

Like most people, my early school experience left a few other "radiators" in my life. It left things I'd rather forget but can't find the strength to remove so I've learned to live with them. Puberty was simply an addition to an already growing list. I was already awkward before hair started sprouting out of my armpits. I towered six feet at the mere age of eleven. The first twelve years of my life I grew seventy-two inches. The past thirty-something I've grown four. Obviously a seventy-two inch sixth grader has trouble with coordination. To put it lightly, I was like a carnival stilt walker but with hinges. Twelve years later I evolved into a machine of eloquent motion but back then I was like a skinny, weak, drunk Godzilla running into things.

Like most young men I stumbled into pornography. I'd sit in my bedroom with a few magazines that made me feel a little less lonely and a little more accepted during a difficult period of growing up. I guess several young men followed this path of initiation into the world of sex, but for me it was more like a hazing. It separated sex from love, which I learned was like separating the fish from the pond. What it did was confuse me in my search, causing me to

78

waste time and hurt people, even myself. Sexuality was a huge deal in middle school, especially when you have a guy named Eddie running around the locker room.

Eddie looked like he was a twenty-four year old boxer on steroids. I think Eddie had failed seventh grade seven times. He wore glasses so thick his eyes looked like they were bigger than his head. Intelligence wasn't his strong point so he enjoyed being an anatomy comedian instead. He basically terrorized my gym class with his threats of violence and cruel jokes about manhood size. Because of Eddie, no one dared to shower no matter how much we sweated. Making it through seventh grade P.E. with Eddie was like surviving Mt. Saint Helens with a mouth full of ash: you were breathing but you had a bad taste in your mouth.

Adolescence is like a slow boil. Life gradually heats up and the skin of childhood peels off like a snake preparing us for something bigger...and hopefully better. It isn't a cruel joke life plays on us. It's more like preparation for the next phase. We aren't made for soup and if we aren't careful this fragile time in life can lead to disaster. This is a time where we often decide how much of our childhood we will move forward, how many of our dreams we will take with us, and how much of our heart we will open to others.

There isn't much about adolescence I really care to remember. But then again, there isn't much I think I will ever forget. There are those memories of smoking three cigarettes, looking at a few lewd magazines, and lying to my parents. Yet there are also memories of feeling an intense battle for my heart, and although I knew I wasn't winning, I felt as if someone was trying to help me fight. I might have crawled away wounded, but I am fairly certain I survived because this someone had a plan for me, even if it did take me half my life to find out who He was. I just never expected him to be a Chicken Whisperer.

"Oh, life is like that. Sometimes, at the height of our revelries, when our joy is at its zenith, when all is most right with the world, the most unthinkable disasters descend upon us."

...from the movie A Christmas Story

CHICKS

My squirrel infested house also comes with five acres of grass, a kid's dream, an adult's nightmare. When a kid has a big yard it is like having a Ferrari—all your friends think you're cool. When an adult has a big yard (to mow) it's like walking around Wal-Mart with your fly open—all your friends think you're an idiot.

Growing up in the country, my yard not only had a lot of grass, but also an interesting collection of wooden sheds and farm animals. It became the center of neighborhood child activity in spite of my mother's insistence that we were killing her mutt grass (no distinct bloodline but considered precious) by walking on it.

My yard had one problem: the clover attracted bees. Walking barefoot across my yard in the summer was like using a wasp nest for a teddy bear: you were asking for it. Luckily the bees were replaced at dusk with a sky of lightning bugs suspended above a carpet of frogs and crickets. With flashes and chirping came hours of safe barefoot running. But all good things must end.

A wire one June night brought an abrupt end to our myth of safe nighttime running and introduced us to our mortality by sending

Tate Lancaster to the emergency room minus one nipple. I've always heard death gets you one piece at a time.

We had a clothesline in my backyard my Dad had rigged so a circus elephant could walk across it. He accomplished this by setting four poles in concrete and reinforcing them with a couple of taunt guide wires pulled as tight as banjo strings. To make a long story short, I knew to duck but Tate tried to play a little music. It took a nice big piece of skin off, including a teat.

Later that night, chest wrapped in bandages, he came back looking for his shoe. After a short search, we determined a dog must have taken it. Two months later I found it. It was on top of my house. If we would have had it on video, we would all be rich, and Tate could have afforded plastic surgery.

Chase anybody and you assume certain risk. But unlike cartoons, the wounds are real. Unlike cartoons, nobody laughs. The world is full of wounded people.

Some say pets are good therapy for wounded people. I think anybody who has a pet, should be paid hourly by the government. Because of my farm experience, I know that raising animals requires constant attention to detail: watering, feeding, cleaning etc. Whereas most kids would love so many pets, I just saw animals as chores. I preferred the chickens and the cows simply because they seemed to give me more bang for my buck- eggs and chicken tenders, milk and steak. In spite of my tendency to eat chickens, they taught me a lot about compassion and heartbreak.

I was excited when I got twenty-five chicks for a 4-H project because I needed the money from egg sales. I had heard if you fed chickens cornbread laced with hot sauce they would shoot a dozen eggs a day out of their butt. At that rate of egg production I was thinking I could save enough money for a red Corvette before I turned sixteen.

My hot rod project started with me keeping twenty-five of the furry little things warm in an incubator and feeding them everyday. Only one would let me poke my finger through the screen and pet it. All the others ran for their life because they could smell Kentucky Fried Chicken on my hands.

My friendship with my lone chick grew quickly and I began to believe my calling in life might be to become a chicken whisperer. For several days my yellow friend was in the exact same spot every afternoon waiting for an afternoon rub. Eventually I started noticing it was the runt and barely growing at all. Two days later I rubbed him a little harder and he fell to pieces- literally. He was dry rotted. The reason he was always standing still is because he was dead, impaled on a piece of wire.

This chick became an omen for the next twenty years of my life: I'd love something and watch it fall apart. Me trying to figure out love on my own was like trying to train a chicken: it didn't work.

It was sad that I fell in love with a dead chicken. I think people love a lot of dead things. We migrate toward the smaller challenge. Love a car- simple, inanimate, temporary, unresponsive, or love a person- complicated, living, eternal, emotional. We like the smaller challenge because it appears safe and it is easy to get our hands on. We assume certain risks when we love the living, but at least we're not petting a dead chicken.

So you can only imagine how excited I was when I found this book in my attic and remembered its author, the Chicken Whisperer, left a legacy of love and instructions on how to not only avoid petting dead chickens but also how to keep them alive. He understood the great challenge of loving people but at the same time he gave them freedom to not respond. His love was strong but tender, persevering but not forceful, and passionate but unbelievably patient. His love was revolutionary and results are legendary. The Chicken Whisperer believed love was worth the risks. He never played it safe. Some would say the way he lived got him killed. I say the way he loved was the only way to really live.

"To love at all is to be vulnerable. Love anything, and your heart will certainly be wrung and possibly broken. If you want to make sure of keeping it intact, you must give your heart to no one, not even to an animal. Wrap it carefully round with hobbies and little luxuries; avoid all entanglements; lock it up safe in the casket or coffin of your selfishness. But in that casket- safe, dark, motionless, airless--it will change. It will not be broken; it will become unbreakable, impenetrable, irredeemable."

C.S. Lewis

"Well, you gotta listen to me here, okay? You gotta win to get love. Everyone knows that. I mean, that's just life. Look at-- Look at Don Shula, legendary coach. Look at, uh, that Asian guy who holds the world record for eating all those hot dogs in a row. Look at Rue McClanahan from The Golden Girls. All three people, all great champions, all loved."

...from the movie Talladega Nights

THE WISDOM OF HIPPY LETTUCE

Ricky Bobby, played by Will Ferrell in *Talladega Nights*, lived his life according to the rule *"If you're not first, you're last."* It was a comment his Dad made while he was high on marijuana. Ricky Bobby lived his life according to the wisdom of hippy lettuce. I lived mine according to the wisdom of movies.

I don't remember my first tear, my first step, or my first word, but I remember my first crush. She was four foot two, hair blonde like Barbie's, eyes brilliant blue like a crayon, and seventy-four pounds of crazy-cute fourth grader. And she sat in front of me. Stare at anything for a year and you'll fall in love.

Seriously, I found my attraction to a girl weird. I was barely pushing ten, still holding G.I. Joe and The Lone Ranger in high regard, when my heart was pierced by Cupid. I guess I was probably attracted to the idea of having a girl in my life that didn't (like my sisters) frame me, or (like my mother) give me a spit bath on Sunday morning.

The problem was I didn't feel like a winner. And winners got girls. I watched James Bond movies and knew I could never kill anybody. I watched Muhammad Ali and knew I could never intentionally break another man's nose. I watched the Dallas Cowboy's and knew I didn't belong in the end zone. I watched the Boston Celtics and knew I'd never have a trophy on my shelf. To impress girls I used other tactics, which is why I needed four hundred staples. Bigger is better: it worked for the Egyptians.

It was Valentine's Day, my tenth year of life, and I was in love. My eyes were blood shot from staring and my ears were sore from spit baths. Believing it would be pulled by the Goodyear blimp, I constructed a four by three foot valentine heart for the girl with crayon blue eyes. In huge bold letters of glue and glitter I wrote, "I LOVE YOU!", folded it, and stuffed it into nine square feet of envelope. I didn't seal it with a kiss. I sealed it with four hundred staples.

The next day at school, while everybody else was busy going from desk to desk depositing small imprinted candy hearts and cheap impersonal Disney cards, I was in the back of the room checking staples on my "personal touch." While I dragged it down the aisle twenty-six pairs of eyes followed me to her desk, making me feel as if I was asking someone to marry me during halftime at the Super Bowl. I arrived at her seat, glimpsed at her beautiful crayon red face, and draped the giant valentine over her desk. She was speechless. She was overwhelmed. She was "molded." She never told me thank you. She never said it was nice. She never told me anything. Silence is not golden.

What I learned that day is there are a whole lot of stupid things people have to say about love, a whole lot of really dumb ideas. I also learned a lot of people have heard them so much they believe them (I'm not the only one who has gone large). A lot of people believe if you have four hundred white geese on a lake and get a woman in a boat she will leave her fiancé. They believe when you are lonely and walk on the beach at sunset you'll find a personal love letter in a corked soda bottle. And some believe women always smell good and every kiss tastes like candy.

Before you kill me, I like geese and I like the idea of finding a love letter stuffed in a glass Nugrape bottle. I like the idea that women always smell good and every kiss tastes like spearmint Tic Tacs. But the truth is geese fly away when you get close, most love letters on a beach were written by six year olds; women have off days; and some kisses taste of onion. Trying to superimpose someone else's love story on my own set me up for disappointment. Trying to run my love life according to random movie wisdom set me up for decades of being single.

Again, I've realized there is a lot of bad information out there. Much of what I heard wasn't true. Much of what I saw wasn't real. I, like most people, got hurt early. That silence, that fear of no response, kept me quiet. My respect for the animal of love was born when it bit me. My fear of the animal of love was born when it made me bleed.

One theme the Chicken Whisperer had in his life and in his relationships was seeking the truth. He had a firm understanding of the fact that living life based on bad or false information can lead to disaster. He not only warned those he loved about all the deception that has piled up over the years but he also went about setting the record straight. He knew if we are ever to find true love we will have to have a set of accurate directions. And he knew he would have to talk us into letting someone else drive.

While I was working on this chapter Jenna and Lauren, a couple of nice fourth grade girls, told me a bad haircut can ruin your love life. Another one told me that Stuart Little is a great date movie. I guess I had a bad hair cut 'cause it took me a long time to make it to the movies.

STABBED BY LOVE

I could never intentionally break a man's nose, but for the right girl, I could stab him with a pencil.

As you can tell, I'm a movie man. I mined them for instructions on life and love in my early years. Although unreliable for wisdom, most told an entertaining story about a villain, a girl in distress, a hero, and violence.

Living in the country on a farm, I didn't have cable or a VCR when I was young, I had Saturday morning cartoons via rabbit ears. My weekly dose of laughter was the only short, hand drawn collection of movies I was allowed to watch as a child. But rather than trying to rescue a girl, my cartoon friends were always trying to get something to eat (I guess they were hungry). While cartoons were short on females, they made up for it with tons of violence.

Sylvester was trying to eat Tweety but a cage and a grandmother stood in the way. Bugs Bunny was trying to get a carrot but was chased by a stuttering man with a rifle. Yogi just wanted a picnic basket but was constantly beaten by a park ranger. Together they taught me going after what you want might make you a victim of violence, but being funny increases your chances of overcoming the opposition.

89

I first experimented with violence as early as first grade when I defended my Christmas candy with a pair of Snoopy scissors. The first time I used violence to rescue a damsel was when I was in sixth grade and defended the object of my affection with a mechanical pencil.

A girl named Shanie, whose silky hair tended to make me forget about school and think about shampoo commercials, sat two desks in front of me. Between us was a bully who was trying to ruin her Clairol career potential. Rufus had breath that smelled like regurgitated rotten eggs, and, for some odd reason, this foul mouthed boy found pulling her hair amusing. He had no idea she was related to Whitney Houston: she had a bodyguard.

Love is like an injection of steroids to the heart. It leads the white knight into the dark forest, the wounded soldier back to the home front, and the lovesick sixth grader to extreme measures of violence.

I watched him pester her for weeks, maybe even months. Everyday, like clock work, out of nowhere, he would yank her hair because, just like me, he probably had a crush on her. With tears in her eyes, she would beg him to stop and of course he would pretend he was clueless about what was happening. At some point, it occurred to me she was a beauty in distress waiting for a hero.

My weapon of choice was a plastic, red, mechanical pencil loaded with .05mm lead, pumped four times. My target was the side of his neck where there was a rumor of a pressure point that could paralyze a man instantly. Honestly, I didn't even think about that. I just stuck him as if I was Brutus stabbing Caesar in the name of Rome.

Two minutes later he was in the bathroom having an inch of lead pulled out of his neck with a pair of tweezers and I was in the hallway grabbing my ankles. I was asked to explain my stabbing action before my teacher paddled me, so I told her the truth: I did it for love. Looking back between my legs I saw her wipe tears from her face. It was a beautiful story. I'd stab him again, but I'd pump it five times and finish the job.

The search for love is the sixth sense that propels us toward the proposition that life will be easier with a little company. The need to find love is the cup of courage that sends us down the aisle with giant valentines, across the desk with pencils, and into the exciting darkness of another's heart. The search for love is what calls us to the center of other people's lives to sometimes assume the role of gladiator. We may be wounded. We may be maimed. We may be torn. But sometimes we will know victory and sometimes... the crowds will go wild.

The Chicken Whisperer believed in fighting for those we love too. But rather than defining fighting as sticking someone with a pencil, he said fighting is defined by how much we are willing to sacrifice on behalf of the person we care about, how close to their suffering we are willing to crawl, and how determined we are to serve them when they are wounded. Rather than for recognition or applause, he encouraged servanthood as a means of defending those we love.

91

This means that the mere act of loving someone, separated from how they respond, or even *if* they respond, should give us a sense of purpose.

We sometimes get confused and believe that joy only comes from love that is reciprocated rather than simply achieving our own personal potential in the relationship and thus pleasing our heavenly Father. Most of the world's relational suffering comes from disappointment where love is not reciprocated. The Chicken Whisperer said that when we love others we are also loving our heavenly Father, and His love is reciprocated back to us constantly through His Son and the Cross.

The Cross sets the standard for true love, where the Son of God, out of love, dies for sinners hoping they will repent but not forcing them. And He dies not only for sinners, but also because his sacrifice pleases God who loves Him and whom He also loves. God's love for his Son enabled his Son to walk in obedience and love us, just as God's love for us enables us to walk in obedience and love others. Sacrificial love in us is enabled by the power of the Cross. Joy can literally come from simply sacrificially loving and serving people the best we can out of our love and gratitude for our heavenly Father. We cannot control others, nor does God, who can, choose to do so. We can only pray that our pure, selfless, sacrificial love will penetrate the walls of defense that are erected daily by the wounded people we know. And sacrifice is a bold statement in the daily news of the human heart.

"It is not the critic, who counts, or how the strong man stumbled and fell, or where the doer of deeds could have done better. The credit belongs to the man who is actually in the arena, whose face is marred by dust and sweat and blood, who strives valiantly, who errs and comes short again and again, who knows the great enthusiasms, the great devotion, and spends himself in a worthy cause; and if he fails, at least fails while daring greatly, so that he'll never be with those cold and timid souls who know neither victory nor defeat." ...Theodore Roosevelt

Shortly after the birth of his first child, our president lost his wife and, on the same day, his mother a few hours later. The year: 1884. The day: February 14th, Valentine's Day.

FIFTY WINDOWS

My house, the chimney, also has fifty windows. Half of
my house is glass. I use a lot of Windex.

From my upstairs bedroom I have a panoramic view of my small
town of Dyersburg thanks to a tornado and my plethora of
windows. Before I arrived a twister did a little landscaping and
removed the trees obstructing my elevated view of the city. Now I
can see the sunset and the roof of Quick Stop.

All my life I've loved storms. I love rain. I love lightning. I love
wind. I love the fact that when I stand outside during a storm I feel
like I'm surviving something- I feel like a winner. There is a part of
me that feels invincible when lighting strikes something other than
me, as if I am temporarily chosen to live.

Weather presented me the opportunity to escape the monotony
of my daily childhood routine. When it started snowing I would
predict the roof would collapse and encouraged everyone to hide in
a protective pocket near furniture when it happened. I gained a
reputation for being an embellisher of the truth. I once saw thirty
rainbows that no one else saw. I also created quite the scene at my
Aunt's house by running through the kitchen screaming, "THE

94

SWAN MAN JUST GOT STRUCK BY LIGHTNING!" My Uncle quickly rushed outside in the rain to find the driver sitting comfortably in his truck. My sisters teared up thinking the ice cream would melt. It wasn't the truth, but it wasn't boring.

Listening to this adrenaline part of my personality, I enrolled in the meteorology program at the University of Oklahoma my senior year of high school. I wanted to be the crazy guy on the weather channel strapped to a pole, reporting sideways in a hurricane. I wanted to be the idiot filming a funnel cloud from his car with cows hitting the hood. I wanted to understand and respect something that most people fear. I just never thought my first lesson would be about love.

The first time I drove to Oklahoma for orientation all I dreamed about were F-5 funnel clouds and going to college next door to the National Severe Storms Lab. The second time I drove to Oklahoma all I dreamed about was a girl with strawberry blonde hair who had rock hard ballet calves.

Romance is like a big remote control changing the channel. One minute you're watching American Choppers and the next thing you know you are watching that cute chef named Rachael Ray cook blueberry pancakes.

After graduating high school, and before leaving for Oklahoma the next morning, I accompanied some friends to a lake were I sat in the fog and talked to a girl named Cheryl who took ballet lessons.

Two weeks later I was still interested enough to ask her out again. A month later I knew she was the one. I knew it would last forever.

While I was aspiring to become the big MF (master forecaster) another young man was back home aspiring to become her BF (boyfriend). I spent the next two years trying to win her back, and another three trying to pick up the pieces. To those around me it looked foolish, like I was spending a hundred bucks trying to win a ten-dollar carnival prize, but to me it was all I had, it was all I wanted. If you've ever been in love you know what I mean. One hard truth I learned about romance is that sometimes it takes your money and makes you look like a clown. Love hurts. But as Tennyson agreed, it was worth it.

> *I hold it true, what e'er befall;*
> *I feel it, when I sorrow most;*
> *Tis better to have loved and lost*
> *Than never to have loved at all.*
> ......*Alfred, Lord Tennyson*

At first I thought searching for love felt like standing in front of a window during a tornado trying to get an inspiring view of it's majesty while pieces of glass stick in your neck. I thought the only alternative I had was to climb down into the dark, safe basement of life and just listen to the whole house fall apart. But once you've seen one, you want to watch it, you want to chase it, you want to understand it, and you want to feel it. You come to know tornados are rare, and although they may destroy our house, they rarely kill us, and sometimes they take us to Oz.

Just like there is something in a moth that tells it to fly into a flame, there was something in my heart telling me to risk love, to seek to understand its power to give and take. If I played it safe, I knew I would rob myself of an essential ingredient of life. I knew it would be dangerous. Did it matter if it was? Not if I have to have it to live; not if flying into a flame is what I was born to do. My greatest fear was, and is, a fear shared with most people. Thoreau said it best, *"I went to the woods because I wished to live deliberately, to front only the essential facts of life, and see if I could not learn what it had to teach, and not, when I came to die, discover that I had not lived."* To have lived, but not have really lived at all. To have loved, but not have really loved at all. I had to find what I was looking for. I had to know love. I had to look to the Chicken Whisperer.

"Dear Red,

If you're reading this, you've gotten out. And if you've come this far, maybe you're willing to come a little further. You remember the name of the town, don't you? I could use a good man to help me get my project on wheels. I'll keep an eye out for you and the chessboard ready. Remember, Red. Hope is a good thing, maybe the best of things and no good thing ever dies. I will be hoping that this letter finds you, and finds you well.

Your friend, Andy"
...from the movie Shawshank Redemption

DESPERATE ENOUGH TO DIG

Like radiators, cats and I have a bad history. When a cat gets near me my face swells up like a plastic milk jug in July heat and my eyes leak like a five- day-old baby diaper (I'm allergic and wanted you to get the point.)

My sister always loved cats in spite of the fact she had horrible luck at keeping them alive. Snowflake froze to death; Tiger was killed in a fight; and Fishy drowned or something. All of her cats were dyslexic: instead of nine lives they had one-ninth.

In spite of my allergies, I couldn't resist wrestling with the furry felines, and I always paid the price. When they bit me with their teeth or scratched me with their claws, I looked like an inmate who had gotten in a prison fight. When my eyes swelled shut my nose would start running and thirty minutes later, after the discharge dried, my shirt looked like it was attacked by a bunch of snails.

Five years ago an attractive female friend of mine talked me in to taking a wounded black cat off her hands because she couldn't have pets in her apartment. Even though I was allergic, I fell under the spell of a begging, beautiful woman. Sampson caved in too.

The kids at her school who rescued him named him Martin because he was black and they found him during black history month. My sister's luck with cats followed me to Dyersburg because Martin was killed by a raccoon as soon as his leg healed up. Officially Martin never died. We never recovered a corpse. Although I loved Martin, I fed the raccoon the rest of his food. Everyone kept telling me raccoons are dangerous. I think only hungry raccoons are dangerous. Well-fed raccoons act like happy cats dressed like Zorro.

Based on my history with Martin, the obvious answer to a girl at Lowe's offering me a kitten was no. But the kitten was black, my favorite animal color. The girl was blonde, my favorite female color. Plus, Godzilla needed a little competition.

I wanted my cat to be like James Bond: a ladies man but good with weapons. As soon as I brought him home I discovered he was easy to train. I trained him to climb on bare skin, pee on clean sheets, dig in his litter box, bat his feces around like a hockey puck and then lick my face right before he stuck his claw through my eyelid. After two weeks he attacked anything that moved and purred like a high-speed fan when he tasted blood. I thought maybe I had a baby panther on my hands. Why did I put up with it? Because, if history repeated itself, it was only temporary.

The blonde who gave him to me told me he was headed to a farm if I didn't rescue him, knowing good and well I couldn't bear to let that happen. She also knew I missed Martin and my raccoon who had disappeared later when the food did. Like Grizzly Adams, I just needed a little more "wild" company even if I did have to buy Benadryl by the pallet.

Eventually I've decided we could not cohabitate. Our friendship had to wait until heaven where the lion lays down with the lamb and allergic people can eat dandelion, poison ivy salad and wipe their mouth with cat hair napkins. He lived outside for awhile and refused to enter the house. He survived a broken leg and a squirrel fight, plus he shared his food with three raccoons. He lived up to the hype. Recently he has gone missing. I am fairly sure a hawk mistook him for a rabbit. I'd put my money on the fact he did not go easily.

It feels strange how desperate I got for company. I got so desperate I tended to do desperate things. While some people head to the bar or the nearest dance club, I just surfed around *match.com* or scouted the sanctuary for the answer to my prayer.

I used to have a distorted view of relationships. I saw them as something to be collected, an accessory, a notch in my belt, a measure of my importance. As a teenager I tried to drive around in circles and play loud music to attract girls (cruising). I would have been better off wearing a sign that said, "*I'm single,*" and riding the Merry Go Round. I thought the acquisition of more money meant the acquisition of more true friends. I thought it was better to have a thousand friends who barely knew me than two who really did. I thought my life would make sense if I was popular and married to a beautiful woman who smelled good and tasted like Tic-Tacs (or chocolate).

I don't believe it is sacrilegious to look for love in the sanctuary but probably a better place to look is on our knees. However, apart from the fact this is primarily a place for worship and not shopping, it would appear my chances of finding a godly woman would go up. Plus the women are arranged in rows and are easy to review if you sing in the choir. If a fellowship follows, you can even tryout their green bean casserole skills.

Like I've already confessed, I also tried the match.com approach. It seemed harmless to post my picture on a dating website. At least I didn't post my prom picture like a lot of other desperate people. It seemed harmless until my sister called laughing and told me her coworker thought I was cute. Harmless until I began to attract the wrong kind of fish. I was going after grouper but I caught carp. I abandoned the internet all together after getting a wink from flatbottomgirl438.

Now half way through my life, I believe relationships are the main course in life; I believe fostering a few is better than maintaining a million; and I believe a marriage for love and laughter is better than a marriage for sex and status. I imagine most of the world is also longing for more meaningful relationships in their lives. We have traded brotherhood and sisterhood for casual acquaintances, sacrificed long-term investment for variety, and settled for a weak, watered down version of romance.

We are craving to be known. We want to fit into a story bigger than us but a story that involves us. We are dreaming of once upon a time, of the garden where true love began, of the place where our hearts were once truly home.

In the movie *Shawshank Redemption* shortly after having received news their friend Brooke had hung himself, Andy told Red to *"get busy livin' or get busy dyin'."* Desperation is a catalyst for change. It is what comes to us in our prison of mediocrity and whispers, *"Escape."* The answer is not to tie our bed sheets together and climb up on a chair. The answer is to come up with a plan for living, to change our perspective of love, and start slowly digging through the walls of bad information and sawing through our bars of bad experiences. The plan is to escape. The plan is to live. The plan is to love better.

*"You know, I once read an interesting book which said that most people lost in the wild, they die of shame. **What?** Yeah, see, they die of shame, 'What did I do wrong? How could I have gotten myself into this?' And so they sit there and they...die. Because they didn't do the one thing that would save their lives. **And what is that?**........... .Think."*

...*from the movie The Edge*

PREPARED TO
CUT MY ARM OFF

The first time I watched *The Edge* I was riding on a bus with forty-four people about to go on an eight mile over night hike in the rain. I was their fearless, clueless leader. The movie was about three men who survive a plane crash in the Alaskan wilderness and then fight for their lives as they try to find help while being stalked by a bear. Ironically, a few hours later, two people in our group found themselves in a similar situation.

We began our hike in a gentle rain, that became a steady downpour, that turned into a flash flood. While the rain complicated our sleeping arrangements, it did little to dampen our spirits...until we lost Dustin and Luke the next morning. For the next forty-eight hours an intense search was conducted with helicopters, all terrain vehicles, and enough manpower to find a needle in a haystack. Luckily, while the flooded river was being dragged for their bodies, they emerged on a logging road and were safely rescued. They were hungry but unharmed, having resorted to using love notes to start a fire and rationing their supplies of gum and cigarettes.

Being lost is a scary thing. When I was seven years old at a family reunion I wandered off down a trail through the woods. Thirty minutes later I looked around and found myself standing in the middle of a forest with no path in site. Panic stricken, I took off running. I panicked because I knew I was about to miss an incredible meal of potluck if I wasn't back in ten minutes. Half an hour later, in tears, I burst through the woods onto a highway. Luckily, an elderly couple stopped and escorted me back to the family reunion just in time to get a piece of Mississippi Mud cake.

In reflection, although I was motivated by hunger, I had no plan. I panicked and was rather lucky my ordeal came to a quick, safe conclusion. At the time I felt like someone started a *"death by starvation timer"* and said, *"Go"*. I estimate I randomly ran somewhere around three miles through the woods that day. If I had not panicked I probably could have simply turned around and walked three hundred yards back to the front of the line for the first serving of baked macaroni and cheese.

When I turned thirty-five it felt like someone started a *"your life's half over, and you will not matter"* timer. And I knew whether or not my life mattered would ultimately be based primarily on my legacy of love toward others and maybe by the laughter I leave behind. Although I had a thousand casual conversations everyday, the deeper, more sincere, *"What is your biggest fear? When is the last time you felt loved? What makes you feel like you matter?"* conversations were rare occurrences. I was totally aware that my own selfishness had contributed to my shallow isolation. I had broken my own cardinal rules of never living alone, being mentored, and meeting weekly with a group of peers to discuss life and God. I used the excuse that I was too busy, and, like a ship not moored to the dock, I slowly drifted out to sea. Alone, with my bearings lost, I had to ask, *"Now what? What can I do? What are my chances?"* I had to think. I had to chart a course, not necessarily back, but rather to where I really wanted to go. Could I build a fire and wait for someone to wander through the woods of my life? Or, since I still wanted to marry the perfect girl, could I shoot a flare gun and use smoke to signal, *"Man down. Send Woman!"* I was convinced of one thing and it wasn't conventional survival wisdom: me finding my way out was dependent on me first finding God again.

I love to read survival stories about people who overcome incredible odds. When I was growing up, I would always grab a *Reader's Digest* on my way to the bathroom and sit and read about survivors until my legs went numb. There were always stories of climbers stuck on mountains, shipmen afloat at sea, and pilots crashing into mountains. Although they often bore the scars of their tragedies (limbless, blind, or disfigured) their post survival attitude reaffirmed the belief that what doesn't kill you makes you stronger. People who survive a tragic event and overcome the odds have a few things in common:

1. They were a victim of a tragedy.
2. That tragedy almost killed them.
3. While wounded, they did something that improved their chances of living.

4. In spite of their injuries, they view the event as positive. (Taylor Swift turned heart ache into millions)

5. They were motivated by something other than their own survival.

Survivors muster the will to live and piece together a plan to prolong their life in spite of the odds being stacked against them. They adapt to sudden changes in their life by making difficult sacrifices. One recent survivor story talks about a man sawing off his own trapped arm, enabling him to escape starvation. In the book *Alive,* several plane crash survivors resort to eating the flesh of their friends who died in the initial crash. They developed a "whatever it takes" approach to surviving. The Chicken Whisperer had the same idea. He even said that sacrificing critical parts of our life that interfere with our ability to love is a good idea. He said that no matter how important it seems, if it is bad for our heart, it must be removed.

Our heart can be broken, it can be bruised, it can bleed...and it can heal. Eight years ago my mother underwent bypass surgery to correct the fact that her arteries were clogged. They cut her down both legs from her inside thighs to her ankles to harvest veins. They then cut her below her throat to her bellybutton and took a saw and separated her breastbone. For the next six hours they rewired her heart. When she emerged from surgery on a gurney there wasn't any sign of life. The ventilator was keeping her alive. The next twenty-four hours were a nervous touch and go period of waiting for her heart to resume its instinct for pumping. Joan of Arc survived and has now dedicated herself, year round, to assembling shoeboxes for Operation Christmas Child. If I have candy at my house she picks it up and says, "*I need this for my shoeboxes.*" The heart and the human body are wonderfully resilient. A true survivor never gives up. A true survivor gets help. A true survivor gets comfortable with change and is willing to undergo dramatic, life saving surgery.

I cannot let fear rule my heart. I cannot afford to panic. I dare not just sit here and die. A plan for healing and change is critical. The tragedy is not that my relationship with others and God is less than what I want; the tragedy would be if I chose to do nothing about it.

Years ago young women anticipating marriage and life on their own would collect things for their future in what was called a hope chest. The chest was typically built by their father or handed down from generation to generation. The chest was usually lined with cedar as a protective barrier against moths. Inside the chest were usually things like linens, dishware, a special dress, and jewelry- all things used by a woman in her new married life. I guess in a way the rest of this story is my hope chest- things I can use to deepen my love for my Father and for my friends. It is my way of pursuing my dreams, my way of protecting the things dear to me, and my way of thinking and hoping out loud for loving better. It is my plan and promise to God and myself.

Hope is more than faith in a better future. Hope is the subconscious heartbeat of eternity in our hearts. My busy life often suppresses its faint cry. But if I allow myself the gift of becoming

107

still, the heartbeat becomes a thunder I cannot escape. I feel its undeniable power to remind me I was meant to know love, deeply and forever. I almost force myself to push the idea of eternal love aside when I suffer the pain of rejection, the disappointment of death, or the slow suffocation of maintaining a thousand superficial relationships. My wounded life becomes a lonely life. But even if I choose to stop loving, I never stop being loved. And this is something important I learned from the Chicken Whisperer.

He said the saddest thing about the people he loved was that they never understood God's love for them has inertia; once put in motion it stays in motion. God's eternal love for us is never dependent on our love for Him or our response. Our response only determines how His love impacts us. God's love for us has initiative; we only love Him because He first loved us. While we have the freedom to be in or out of a relationship with God, we are never out of his love. One of the unique things about God is, unlike us, He loves out of his nature, not in response to affection, whereas we love Him in response to his affection for us.

The more I read about the Chicken Whisperer it becomes clear he fully grasped God's love for him. His understanding of God's love enabled him to be constant in his love for others under difficult circumstances because God's love for him sufficiently met his need of affirmation. He was very upset about the fact that people felt unlovable. It is one thing to believe no one loves you and quite another to believe there is nothing in you to ever love. The Chicken Whisperer had a reputation of giving the people who thought there was nothing in them to love his special attention. He wrapped his arms around people others pushed away. He employed people others fired. He praised people others cursed. His love was radical, revolutionary, and redemptive. His love is what saved my life.

"And when you get down to it, Lily, that's the only purpose grand enough for a human life. Not just to love--but to persist in love." Sometimes loving people isn't easy. They may push you away because they don't love themselves enough to trust your love, or they have been hurt before and are protecting their hearts. And, then there are those who just plain do not feel the same way about you as you feel about them. How do you know? Perhaps the answer is to offer love to everyone, not expecting anything in return. A jealous, covetous love can be harmful to both people causing one to be smothered and the other rejected. On this journey we call life, we all have a purpose. It is to learn to love and love well."

...from the movie The Secret Life of Bees

IN OUR OWN INTEREST TO BE INTERESTED IN OTHERS

I have two aunts who are twins. Debbie is married to a retired chemist/piano restorer and sings in the choir at church. Her twin, Donna, is single and lives in an assisted living facility. Donna lived a fairly normal life until about the age of thirty when she was diagnosed with schizophrenia after suffering through a rather painful divorce. After the divorce, she lived alone for several years passing the days by rearranging furniture and doodling. She lived without a television and received no news of what was going on in the world. She was oblivious to who was President, the terrorist's attacks of 911, or the computer revolution. Over time, she disintegrated into poor health with long gray hair and dental problems. In isolation, Donna aged twice as fast as Debbie. Side by side, the twins looked completely different.

One day Debbie went by to take Donna her weekly groceries. She found her in the rain lying outside on the ground bleeding from her head. When Donna had gone to toss the trash off the back porch she forgot to let go.

The family decided it was time for Donna to live in an assisted living facility. Inside her new community a dramatic and wonderful change took place. She started caring about herself again. She cut her hair, got her teeth fixed, and began to respond better socially. Being around people was good for her health.

I also need hard to find and hard to develop relationships in my life. I need fragile friends, I need fragmented family, and I need to belong to a complicated community. I need someone other than myself for myself because there is a piece of me, that exist outside of me, that only someone else can reveal to me.

Relationships are like mirrors revealing who I really am. They clue me into the fact I have a stray back hair, a button missing, or need to pluck my eyebrows. They reveal I have too much of a temper, too little patience, and not enough compassion. Relationships give me helpful feedback by how people respond to my words and actions. Maintaining and growing these delicate relationships forces me to exercise my love muscles and ensures my heart is healthy.

Long before John Donne wrote, *"no man is an island entire of itself,"* another author called Moses recorded that God said the same thing.

God saw that one lonely, naked man sitting in the Garden and knew it wasn't a good thing. And so He gave him a little company.

I've always thought it was interesting how God used a piece of Adam to make Eve when He had the capacity to just start from scratch. My grandmother always saved a little yeast dough to seed the next bread batch (I knew she took her cues from a higher power). I think God might have done it this way to symbolically connect the two, stressing the fact that it was in their own interest to cherish and love a satellite part of their self. I imagine if I knew a girl was running around with my finger on her hand, I would have an interest in keeping her alive because I might want my finger back. Seriously, it must have been the strangest and dearest thought to wake up and realize Eve was literally a part of his own flesh and blood and that it was in his own interest to be interested in someone else.

This idea that it is in our own interest to be interested in others is a simple but radical idea. If I look after your interest, then you are free to look after my interest. And just who is in a better position to look out for someone? The other person of course! We can't see behind us; we can't even see our own face; we can't look at our life from an unbiased point of view. We are held hostage by our own blinding set of circumstances. The idea of having a partner is brilliant. The idea of having a partner who is self absorbed is sad.

At first I used to think I needed a fancy bike, a cool backpack, and ice cream money. As a child I could see Mickey needed Minnie (because no one else could tell what he was saying) and Kermit needed Ms. Piggy. Oscar lived by himself in a trashcan because he was a grouch. Superman needed Lois Lane and Spiderman turned out to need Kirsten Dunst (I thought I needed her too). The Incredible Hulk never had a steady girlfriend and had an anger problem. I could see it years ago: being alone makes you green.

I used to work the relationships in my life to move in the direction of getting the things I wanted. But life has taught me what I need is to find out what others need, and to work the relationships in my life to move in that direction. I have learned that it is in my interest to be interested in others.

One reason I tend to be self-centered is because I sometimes believe the lie that life is a competition. I fall into the trap of getting my identity from what I do or what I have and comparing myself to my neighbors rather than getting my identity from whom my Father is. With the presumption that I must win, or at least perform well, I become absorbed with self-promotion and self-preservation. Rather than contributing to the people around me and encouraging them to make their own contribution, I sometimes try to conquer or dominate them and call it "leading."

I used to think a good friend of mine had said, "*Comparison is the thief of joy,*" but actually it was C.S. Lewis. This is probably the smartest thing a human being has ever uttered. Comparison turns community into competition and friends into foes. Comparison is an act of self-mutilation practiced daily by people who are overwhelmed by the need to fit in. Through comparison I collect the tiny pressures of life and carry them around as if they are my security blanket, when in reality, they are a noose pulled tighter around my heart.

All this comes out of fear, the fear of being left behind, the fear of being left alone. I stood in line early in life wincing at the thought that no one would pick me for their team. And this fear grew with rejection, with heartache, and with loss. The irony is my personal response to the fear of being alone made me unbearable to be around. No one RSVP's to a pity party and a self-promoter is simply annoying. In the pursuit of popularity I often wounded or wore out those whose approval I sought. The sad thing is while I may have offended or hurt people in the process, I truly just wanted to be loved. The irony is I need to feel loved first to free me up to love those around me. I need to feel loved to overcome the fear to love. It's like a relational standoff: if you love me, I'll love you, but who's going to love first? And when I understood what was happening, I felt inclined to humble myself and take the risk of going first.

The idea of humbling myself and serving others stood in direct contrast to the idea of being a winner. Now I can see a dominating point of view destroys true community. I think true community is when everybody feels equally valued, appreciated, and important. The fruit of true community is humility and selflessness; a group of people who understand it is in their interest to be interested in others, a group of people who love each other.

114

"Do nothing out of selfish ambition or vain conceit, but in humility consider others better than yourselves. Each of you should look not only to your own interests, but also to the interests of others."

Philippians 2:3-4

I believe the secret to building true community is for everyone to have one person in their life that loves them unconditionally, a person who knows everything about them but still looks them in the eye and says, *"You're OK."* Because the Chicken Whisperer always felt loved by his father, he was able to navigate great periods of struggle in his other relationships. Again, if we know we are loved, we are prepared to love others, even when they don't appreciate or acknowledge our affection. Having one great relationship enables us to have the patience to work on deepening other relationships.

Sometimes we approach relationships only for what we can get, not for what we can give. The ideal approach would be to go in wanting to give, wanting to help, and wanting to make the other person feel loved. Sometimes we will enjoy being loved back but sometimes we will learn that true love is born in compassion and reared in sacrifice; we will learn that relationship, community, is hard work. Yet, denying our heart the opportunity to risk love is not playing it safe; it is playing it selfish, and ironically the person who eventually gets hurt the most is the one who risks the least.

The Chicken Whisperer said it might help to think of loving others as loving our self, or to remember our own needs and struggles when reaching out to other people who are wounded. When we throw the football we should think about how we would

115

want it thrown to us. Another great idea is what his father once said. He said it is worse to love someone and never tell them than it was to chew someone out publicly. Unspoken love kills community faster than arguments. We should understand the main need of people around us is to feel loved, that our main need is to feel loved, and our main goal is to tell the people that matter to us how much we love them. By doing this we set them up to love better, to even love us more. It is in our own interest to be interested in others.

116

"When I was a kid, my father had this dog that started to get all weak and sickly. He takes it to the vet; he examines it and says a maggot must have laid eggs in the dog's butt. The baby maggots have crawled up, now they've started to grow, and eventually they're gonna eat the dog alive from the inside. He says it should be put to sleep, because it's an old dog anyway. But father won't do it. He takes the dog home, he puts it on the bed, he reaches up into the dog, picking out the maggots with his finger, one by one. It takes him all night, but he gets every last one. That dog outlived my father. That's love, Sam.

... from the movie Addicted To Love

WHO'S YOUR DADDY

Our definition of love is often shaped by where our heart has been. Much like how when I eat at El-Patio I smell like Mexican food or when I've been to Java Cafe I smell like coffee, our heart is embedded with the aroma of our past. Our heart is both a memorial and a current affair, an assembly of prejudices and inclinations based upon both truth and lies. Like a wounded animal that will bite the hand that feeds it; the wounded heart cannot always be trusted by its owner. If we seek true affirmation it must come from the outside, it must come from God.

While growing up I liked fishing, I had an affair with candy, but I loved my dog. Charlie was an adorable mutt that looked like a worn-out black and white bathroom rug. He liked peanut-butter sandwiches and day old scraps but wouldn't pass up the chance to feast on road kill if it was warm. Charlie and I shared a common enemy: the school bus. The yellow monster interrupted my summer vacations and tried to make a rug out of Charlie twice. He did what I wanted to do: chased, barked, and tried to bite the tires.

We were on a family camping trip at Loretta Lynn's when I got the news that my father had shot and killed Charlie, something about worms. It was a difficult night of crying in my sleeping bag wondering how my loving father could have shot my best friend. He was the only animal I have ever felt like I loved. He was the only animal whose loss made me cry. And very early in life I associated love with loss and tears.

Because we simply couldn't afford the vet, I now understand my father actually acted in a very loving way by ending Charlie's pain, but back then I doubted his judgment. I didn't necessarily believe eating too many cookies would stunt my growth or sitting too close to the television would give me cancer either. My parents who said they loved me just seemed to be taking the fun and friends out of life. The dual role of loving and protecting is confusing to a child, especially a child looking for affirmation. When I try to understand the dilemma of parenting I think about a friend of mine, Josh Walden, who was recently on a foreign mission trip to the Dominican Republic.

While enjoying his last day on the beach with other university students, a few of his friends waded out from the beach into very large waves and, unknowingly, a very dangerous rip-tide current. The next few minutes unraveled into a fight for their lives while they frantically swam for shore. One of his friends, Shane Ruiz, was unable to break free from the rip tide and was dragged out to sea. For the next three hours his friends and others tried to reach him but the large waves kept pushing them back. Shane's body was never recovered.

In many ways parents must feel how Josh and his friends felt while they painfully watch the child they love fight for their lives. They want to help but sometimes there is nothing they can do. There is indeed a terrible ocean of circumstances that make the task of parenting difficult. While some parents have the benefit of having been raised by strong "swimmers," others simply reflect the weaknesses of their own upbringing. Some are able to overcome their inadequate childhood and establish new patterns of affirmation and love in their own families, while for others the wounds received in their childhood reemerge in painful waves that negatively impact their own children. I personally feel like my parents overcame their personal childhood challenges but I realize for many it simply feels as if their parents never attempted to save them, and for some even still, that their parents held them under water. While parents may be limited in their ability, we must also remember they are trying their best to balance guidance with affection which is a difficult task. As a matter of fact, often the pressure to raise a productive child is so overwhelming the parents often forget the power of affection and affirmation and instead focus on discipline and training, or even worse, they do nothing. Missing the critical affirmation and affection of a parent, the child walks into other relationships in life crippled, drudging along with low self esteem, or often with pain masked either in anger or self pity.

In these critical years of childhood we are also beginning to define love. What does it mean to love somebody? What does love feel like? What does love look like? And we get some pretty bad answers. For the girl whose father whispers "*I love you,*" as he molests her, love is a painful surrender of control. For the boy whose

119

parents gave him everything but time, love is the cheap substitution of expensive things. For the kids whose parents appeared to set on the sideline when pornography ripped a hole in their heart, when alcohol attacked them like a cancer, or when they painfully exhausted themselves chasing popularity, love is passive. And we incorrectly superimpose our poor definition of love and less than perfect experience of our earthly parents onto God our heavenly Father. Corrupting the character of God with the infusion of our poor earthly experiences is a huge, but common, mistake.

Rose and I were hanging out at Java Cafe when I started thinking through what love is and how our experiences play a huge role in what we expect and what we aim for.

Two of prettiest girls I know are Blackberry and Rose. I've known them both for almost ten years and I've watched them ripen on the vine, having grown up into wonderful maturing Christian women. They both, in some way, struggled with missing the voice of affirmation from their earthly father and the wound was deep causing them a large amount of pain. While some of the pain was the simple feeling that their father never brought himself to bear, they admit much of the pain came from the collateral damage of moving from guy to guy looking for the missing piece. Their fragile hearts were broken many times leaving them struggling with deepening feelings of insecurities.

Rose is probably my favorite female in the world. I call her Rose because she migrates toward "Titanic" challenges. She dug down deep a couple years ago and figured out she could run a marathon and survive without eating meat. Her body is a well-oiled machine and her hair reminds me of a shampoo commercial. Her heart is soft like cotton but she can be amusingly stubborn like plastic wrap on cds sometimes. She jumps on board insurmountable challenges like biking 100 miles as if it was a simple matter of will power and then tries to recruit me for these voyages of death. When I bring up the facts that we struggled to make a few laps around downtown Dyersburg and that my cushion was sore for three days, she simply reminds me of the fact that Lance Armstrong is proof of the possibility while totally ignoring the obvious icebergs in our path, icebergs like Timmy has no cushion on his tushion.

Although she is beautiful, she hasn't always felt beautiful and even went as far as struggling with an eating disorder which might be a product of that missing affirmation from her father, or the absence of feeling truly loved at times. It is so strange to watch a beautiful woman like Rose struggle with her body image but in the story of the ugly duckling we are reminded how missing a critical piece of information about our self leads to the irony of the majestic swan believing he is a misfit among mallards.

All our lives we are either trying to get love or give love. Our definition of love, especially in childhood, is either slowly formed, or distorted, primarily by our interactions with relatives. Depending on how close these relationships reflect the true and pure love of God they can either equip us or cripple us. In the absence of affirmation the question of "what's wrong with me" lingers. This

121

question must be answered, or the crippled heart will inappropriately, under the disguise of interest, try to earn approval. Thus the relationship constantly teeters on maintaining a certain level of approval. Whereas a God affirmed person simply loves for the joy of loving, the doubting heart's enjoyment of love is shifted to anticipation of how well the other person responds. This is tragic. A myriad of circumstances can limit or even completely eliminate any response. And more often than not these circumstances are not even related to the doubting heart's efforts. If my business is failing, I will not be enthusiastic about a great dinner. If my stomach is hurting, I will not be enthusiastic about a great dinner. If I do not like asparagus, I will not be enthusiastic about asparagus casserole. None of these are negatives related to the person preparing the meal but can be received in such matter because a certain level of approval is absent. The success of the relationship almost depends on the world being perfect. With affirmation the heart is set free to love within a world that it less than perfect. The discovery of true love is life changing; enabling a once doubting heart to become a spring of living water.

The Chicken Whisperer not only understood love, he defined love. The Chicken Whisperer had a great father. And the outside affirmation that came from his father enabled him to do something amazing: it allowed him to affirm you, me, and all of God's other children, it allowed him to love us completely and deeply, it allowed him to free us from doubt and enter into the joy for which we were created. Jesus is the Chicken Whisperer.

Jean Valjean: When you're better, I'll find work for you.
Fantine: But you don't understand, I'm a whore... and Cosette has no father.
Jean Valjean: She has the Lord. He is her father. And you're his creation. In his eyes, you have never been anything but an innocent and beautiful woman.

...from the movie Les Miserables

THE FATHER'S LOVE

I heard a story once that talked about a man who had several wild birds he cared for and fed daily. A particularly hard winter made it difficult for the birds to find the food he would leave for them. They would fly to the man's back door looking for the food he had scattered on the ground but the falling snow would have covered it up. The man noticed this and grabbed more food to give to them as they arrived but when he opened the door to scatter the bread they were frightened and flew off. The man would quickly go back inside and the birds would slowly return but by then the food was again covered by the snow. Sadly, the man looked out of the window at the hungry birds who he loved deeply. And then he said to himself, *"If only I could become a bird to bring them food then they wouldn't fear me and they would live."*

The radical idea of changing our nature or behavior to approach and influence a different species is called "whisperering" because of its gentle approach. The idea of "whisperering" an animal is to keep it calm and available for interactive training by making it feel safe through soft touch and gentle gestures. Many animals have been successfully trained in just a few hours using this method as opposed to harsher more brutal methods. Jesus was God's way of whispering mankind.

"O Jerusalem, Jerusalem, you who kill the prophets and stone those sent to you, how often I have longed to gather your children together, as a hen gathers her chicks under her wings, but you were not willing! "

.... *Jesus*

These words were part of a lengthy sermon Jesus delivered in the Temple warning those there about giving false teachings about God. And He gets heated delivering a scorching sermon about the abuse inside the leadership of the church and then suddenly, out of nowhere, he talks about gathering his children under his wing to protect them. The heart of God is broken over what is happening to his children.

We are timid like wild horses. Our spirits have been spooked and damaged by horrific events in our history. Our hearts have become frail and broken from the abuse and abandonment of our own species. We now fear with a great sadness the day our great majestic Father returns. We fear His disappointment. We fear the absence of His love. While we have heard He can save us, we doubt that He will want to. We are starved for His affection, but believe it will be withheld. But He comes, and He comes to us how only a loving Father could...as a Son.

The holy night He comes the long silence is broken by the voice of an angel saying, *"Do not fear, I bring you news of great joy to all people..."* And then we find him, our Redeemer, weighing merely eight pounds, helpless, hungry, and in our image. Into our arms comes a tiny child of promise, a child who will save us, a child who can whisper the intimate things of a loving Father to his lost children, a child who we do not fear.

Our fear of the Father is as misguided as our doubt of his sincere love for us was in the Garden, for the Son did not come to punish but to save. He did not come to wage war but to bring peace. He did not come in anger. He came in love. And in Him we are reacquainted with the heart of the Father we fear. He does not raise his hand against us. Instead He uses his gentle, powerful hands for healing the bleeding woman, restoring the blind man's sight, and washing the feet of his disciples. He does not speak harshly to us. Instead His voice defends children, raises dead brothers, and prays for misguided soldiers. Rather than ruling, our King humbles himself and touches the sick, befriends the sinner, and spares the prostitute. He sits on no throne but rather upon a hill and grieves over the condition of his children. Our Chicken Whisperer weeps, He feels, He loves, and He acts. Before He does what He came to do He reveals a very important truth, "*If you have seen me, you have seen my Father.*" And then on the cross, as the only beloved Son of God exchanges his life for ours, the heart of our Father can no longer be questioned. He is merciful. He is faithful. He is for us.

By openly showing him affection, God empowered Jesus to walk in obedience through difficult circumstances and complete His plan of redemption for mankind which included becoming like us to serve as our representative, fulfilling the law by keeping every commandment as the perfect Lamb of God, and finally by dying as our substitution for the penalty of our sin. Cherishing freedom as an attribute of genuine love, God allows man to choose, man chooses unwisely. God creates a plan to save man but not to control man. God's plan involves creating a powerful reminder that involves a penalty, and then God shocks the world by paying the penalty with the sacrifice of his own Son. God the Father loves us through the Son.

Although I personally felt quite loved as a child, I know there are sad cases of people who grow up in the absence of love; and thus, I began looking for a universal source of affirmation outside of loving parents or a loving childhood. I turned to God the Father. Jesus often talked about his Father, about how he loved his Father, and about how he knew his Father loved him. While I was very blessed with a hardworking father who sincerely had my best interest at heart, I know not everyone was as fortunate as me, and the idea of being affirmed by a father type figure is difficult to approach. The need is to view God from the fresh perspective on his own actions, untainted by our prejudices and opinions based on both bad experiences with people and bad information from unreliable sources. The idea that God the Father loves us and affirms us is equally old news as it is breaking news. But who better to affirm us all than the one who truly knows us? Who better to hear "I love you" from than the One who can love us most deeply?

Feeling loved does a lot for me. It makes me feel wanted, needed, liked, and enjoyed. It makes me feel special, significant, valuable, and important. It makes me feel safe, secure, protected, and partnered. In the absence of feeling loved I would think most of us would feel unwanted, unliked, insignificant, unimportant, unsafe, insecure, and lonely... and I would think it would be very hard to love someone else feeling like that.

In the Wizard of Oz the great wizard said, "*The heart is not judged by how much you love, but by how much you are loved by others.*" Jesus believed the meaning of life was to love God and to love others and all this starts with understanding God's own love for us. In reading his story, it was obvious that by putting this into practice he literally enabled the people around him to love others, or by making them feel wanted, important, and secure (revealing God's love to them), he freed them up to risk an investment in someone else. I guess in a way, what we risk (rejection, sorrow, loss) diminishes in light of the fact that we have this reservoir, or guarantee, that we are already loved.

Jesus said he felt loved by his father his entire life and this incredible love allowed him to take incredible risks. He knew that no matter what happened to him his relationship with his Father was enough in itself to compensate for any losses. Yet, he also knew that by imitating the love of his father, he simply couldn't lose. He believed in love so deeply because he was loved so deeply. He knew love's full potential.

When he willingly died on the cross he did it as much for the joy it gave his father to see him act in obedience as he did it for the joy that it would eventually bring to us. His love for his father was the driving force in his life. True love works like that; your joy is measured by the joy you give the other person. So it also gave Jesus great joy to die for you. And now the Father and Son's joy must be made complete.

"Dear Edward,
I've gone back and forth the last few days trying to decide whether or not I should even write this. In the end, I realized I would regret it if I didn't, so here it goes. I know the last time we saw each other, we weren't exactly hitting the sweetest notes-certainly wasn't the way I wanted the trip to end. I suppose I'm responsible and for that, I'm sorry. But in all honesty, if I had the chance, I'd do it again. Virginia said I left a stranger and came back a husband; I owe that to you. There's no way I can repay you for all you've done for me, so rather than try, I'm just going to ask you to do something else for me-find the joy in your life. You once said you're not everyone. Well, that's true-you're certainly not everyone, but everyone is everyone. My pastor always says our lives are streams flowing into the same river towards whatever heaven lies in the mist beyond the falls. Find the joy in your life, Edward. My dear friend, close your eyes and let the waters take you home."
                                                        ....from the movie The Bucket List

COMPLETED JOY

What I am about to tell you changed my life. It happened to me in the midst of writing this book. It was so profound that I literally had a hard time talking about it without crying for weeks. Even now I am tearing up thinking about how it happened.

When I got into the coffee shop business I just knew I had found a gold mine. I started with absolutely no money, and with a little help from family, I opened three stores in six months. I had a great name: Green Frog Coffee Co. I had a great plan: sophisticated but southern. I even had great employees. What I didn't have was a great clue about how expensive it was to start a business. When the finances didn't exactly pile up I ignored critical cash flow problems and kept one rural location open simply because it was aesthetically pleasing, which is like buying a Ferrari that doesn't run. On the outside it looked like I had successfully opened three profitable coffee shops in just a few months and was on the fast track to be to Starbucks what Netflix was to Blockbuster, but I was more like a VHS tape in a Blu-Ray market. In as little as eighteen months, during the Great Recession, I went from $25,000 of structured debt with one store to $350,000 with three stores. I was loosing $10,000 a month and having a difficult time adjusting things to become profitable. I loved sitting in my Ferrari pretending it could run.

The financial pressure had a huge impact on my personality. I was still connecting with people and still attempting to minister by leading small groups, but ultimately, I was adrift spiritually. My time with God was sporadic, my prayers were as rare as rainbows, and I was lonely. A few people reached out to me, but like an idiot, I chose to walk the gauntlet alone, and I paid the price. It wasn't pretty. I became a "clanging symbol." My love suffered.

At first I cloaked my pain and problems and did really good pretending all was well, but then in a span of about six weeks, I did a bunch of stupid stuff. While grilling on a camping trip I acted like a spoiled reality star on a rant when a wasp stung my ear and made it swell up like a fat pancake. Then a few days later, I went on a crazy tare with a vendor about some paper cups as if we were talking about organs that needed to be air-lifted to my mother. And then finally, while cooking out at my house, I smashed a ceramic plate with some metal tongs when someone made a comment about my party gift not being up to snuff. I embarrassed myself and it was a relationship repellent. I was killing what I needed: community. Stress will reduce you to who you really are.

At the time church was hit and miss but this one particular Sunday I stumbled in because I was feeling ashamed about my attendance. I sat in the back. I went because I wanted to show some gratitude because my loan to straighten out my finances had finally gone through and the company was finally turning a profit. I remember singing but more than anything I was thinking, thinking about my life, thinking about how I just felt like I was failing in not only my relationship with God but in every relationship I had. And that is when everything changed.

We take communion every week at my church. Communion is a sacrament of the church that recognizes the death of Jesus Christ and the shedding of his blood for the forgiveness of sins (aka-a demonstration of God's love for the sinner). Typically some type of bread represents his body and some type of juice or wine represents his blood. By eating and drinking these sacraments a person remembers their need for Christ and the depths of the Father's love for them. At our church we get this tiny thimble of juice and an oyster cracker. Usually I hold one in each hand, side by side, and while reflecting on God's love, I pray, "*God teach me to love others like you love others.*" I remember it like it was ten seconds ago. My heart started racing and out of nowhere, as I stared at the sacraments of God's love for me, I prayed, "*God teach me to love you, like you love me.*" And then tears came. And they have never really stopped. For the first time in my life, I believe I understood what God wants: He wants the hand of my heart. God wants me as partner. He wants me to love Him.... because it will enable him to lead me.

"Jesus replied: 'Love the Lord your God with all your heart and with all your soul and with all your mind.' This is the first and greatest commandment. And the second is like it: 'Love your neighbor as yourself.' All the Law and Prophets hang on these two commandments."

Matthew 22: 37-40

Even in the Garden Satan was trying to ruin our love relationship with God by trying to convince us that He had an ulterior motive for creating us other than fellowship, that God was on a power trip when the truth was as plain as the fruit in front of our face. If God wanted control, would He have given us a choice? Although He doesn't want to control, He does want to lead, lead his children into a relationship with love. He wants freewill fellowship.

In the very first part of our story we find our powerful Father bringing his incredible animal creations to us as gifts of love and it gives Him great joy to allow us to name these gifts: giraffe, elephant, ostrich, gorilla, deer, eagle, etc. Can you imagine Adam's excitement? Can you imagine God's joy? But there is one more gift, a gift born out of God's observation of mankind who he loves, a gift so beautiful it trumps every other creation: the gift of woman. The joy is so great it is followed by resting!

Our eternal God who had all knowledge and all power, breathes life into dirt and begins a very intimate interaction with the life He Creates. Obviously God wanted a relationship because he continued to invest in the relationship, even after the story takes a terrible turn.

Here it became evident that He loves us deeply because rather than starting over, He sets about redeeming what is lost, what is loved. And even this act of redemption created fellowship and joy for the Father. *"For God so loved the world that he sent his only Son."*

Jesus said, *"As the Father has loved me, so have I loved you. Now remain in my love. If you obey my commands, you will remain in my love, just as I have obeyed my Father's commands and remain in his love. I have told you this so that my joy may be in you and that your joy may be complete."*

His desire is that we will have joy in our life. God wants you to have joy. (pause) He said that he came that we might *"have life and have it to the full."* God wants your joy to be complete. (pause) And Christ makes this possible. Christ wanted us to experience the same connection to God that he had, the same fellowship, because He knew it is our most critical need. The very thing we were created to do was to connect to the Father. He then said this connection is facilitated through our obedience to God's Word. The commandments that we often view as restrictive fences actually provide a path to fellowship with God and even other people. The commandments enable us to abide in the affirmation of God's love. They create an environment conducive to experiencing God. Like the Golden Rule *"do unto others as you would have them do unto you"*, they are the secret to successful relationships. They increase our ability to love, thus leading us to complete and full joy.

Yet we must make peace with God in our hearts and become obedient to his Word. We must trust the heart of the Father so we can become automatically obedient to Him like sheep following a shepherd they trust. *"My sheep know my voice, and they obey me."* God seeks obedience from his children not so he can simply celebrate our surrender to his power, but rather so he can celebrate our safety. God is not on a power trip. God is on a love trip. A radical thought to set a new perception of God in motion in your heart is ...God is humble. Love does not boast. God, the God of the universe, the God of all power, the God of all knowledge, chooses to live in humility, and this is so attractive to me. When Jesus humbled himself into the likeness of a man and became obedient unto death, he was simply acting within his character. Remember when Moses asked God how He wished to be addressed, God replied, *"I am who I am."* Is that a humble answer or what! God is humble: this one thought exponentially increased my love for God.

Our obedience, our joy, depends on trusting the humble heart of Christ and the loving heart of the Father he came to reveal. Jesus was the *"visible expression of the invisible God."* And what He reveals is as breath-taking as it is comforting. He says our Father's heart is like a woman who loses a coin, lights a lamp, and sweeps the whole house to find it, and when she does she rejoices. He says our Father's heart is like a shepherd who upon finding a lost sheep, joyfully puts it on his shoulders and carries it home (I am crying), there is no kicking the sheep, no hitting it with a stick, no cursing, or dragging it by its neck. And He says our Father's heart is like a father who had a prodigal son who abandoned him, wasted his fortune, and then came crawling home hungry and desperate, but

134

the father has been waiting for his son, and runs to him, embraces him, and kisses him (I am crying very hard), his arms are not folded, there is no scolding, there is no beating, there is no punishment, there is...there is a celebration...in all three stories there is joy. God's joy, and ironically our joy, is complete when we repent and trust, when we are found, when we return to our loving Father, who not only did not spare his own Son, but continues to lovingly and patiently search for those who are still lost. What would happen if we responded to God's love by loving him back? It would complete us, just like it completed Jesus.

So we must decide now that we have the information we need: are we an ugly duckling or are we an elegant swan? The answer will be determined by the voice we listen to. Do we continue to listen to the father of lies and doubt our worth, rejecting the precious gift of God, living a life embellished in sin and destructive relationships, a life devoid of joy? Or do we listen to the voice of our real Father, the Father who loves us, who says we belong in a Kingdom, and who has sent the Prince to rescue us, restore us, and redeem us; a Father who wishes us great joy.

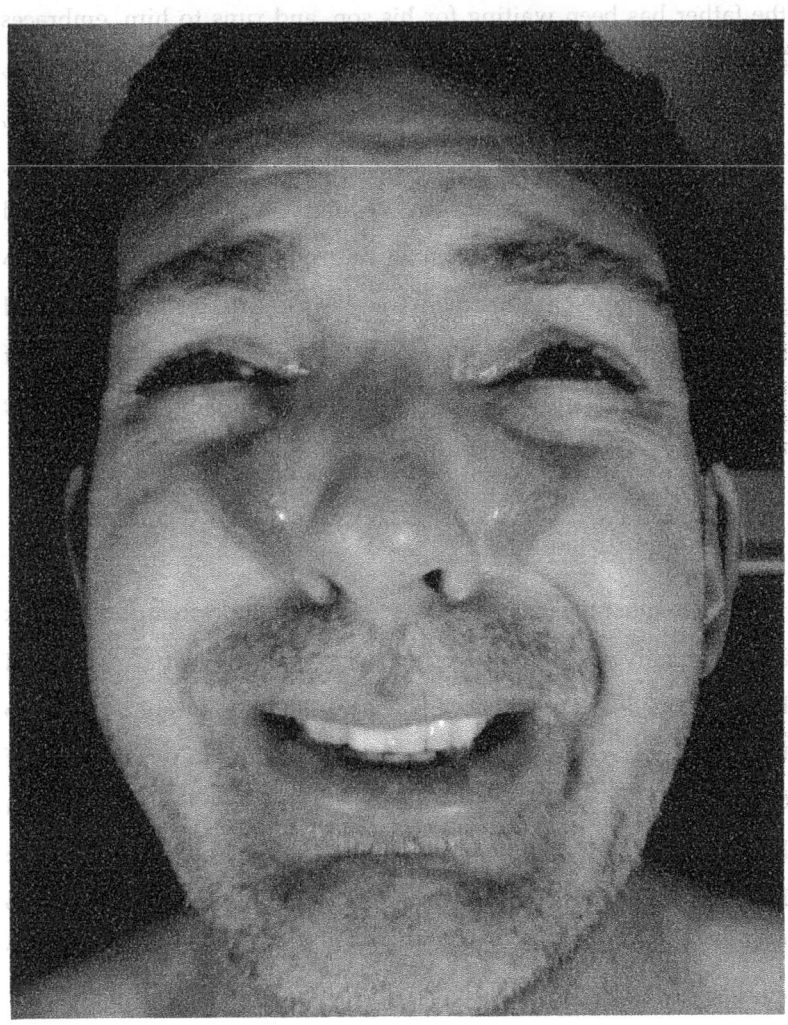

I wanted to share this photo for a very simple reason: to reveal how hard this has been. It has been hard to admit I have ignored the first commandment while focused on the second. And it has been even harder to grasp how much it has hurt both me and God. I am truly sorry for forsaking my first love. It is both a strange and powerful moment to come to the Cross, where you have led others, and find a Savior you haven't truly loved.

"We got the lab reports back this morning. I'm sorry Bob, they don't look very good. There's been no reduction in tumor size or density, and based on your response to the interleukin therapy, I can't recommend further treatment. We're losing ground Bob. The tumor is growing. And I think you have to face things as they are. Of course we'll continue to monitor everything. You could still have three or four months, I think you should aim for that. *Four months? You have a spring to look forward to. The symptoms won't be too bad. We have drugs to manage the pain.* What if I want to do the treatment again? What if I elect to do it, are you going to stop me? Are you going to get a court order to stop me? *I can't believe you are asking this! The interleukin nearly killed you! It was touch and go for six hours. And it didn't work.* Come on. I'm still in the game here man, you know. Come on. One more. There have to be a lot of other therapies, a lot of other treatments, right? *Bob don't make it any more painful than it has to be. You don't have a lot of time left. Don't waste it in futile searches."*

... from the movie My Life

END OF THE SNIPE HUNT

My early experience with love, or what I thought was love, made me doubt happily ever after. It made me wonder if something was wrong with me, or, if something was wrong with God. I didn't know what love was, so trying to find it was like going snipe hunting.

Snipe hunting is a classic southern joke played on the inexperienced camper. My first snipe hunt happened at a boy's church retreat when I was about seven years old. With my pimento loaf sandwich (my mom must have been in a hurry) I arrived at the campout ready for fun but didn't know it would be at my own expense. As rookie campers, several of us were told there were special birds called snipes roosting on the ground in the field next to our campsite that could easily be caught with a paper sack and some fancy whistling. When someone asked what the birds looked like the answer was, *"You'll know one when you catch one."* We were then handed a paper sack, taught how to do the special whistle, and allowed to waste an hour or so running meaningless around the field in the dark, because, of course, the birds didn't exist. A lot of us are hunting for snipe, searching for something that we have no idea what it looks like or even if it really exists. But the futile searching can end with the Chicken Whisperer.

Somewhere within our heart, buried deep beneath the disappointment of dead ends, is a repressed, eternal instinct inclined to the voice of our real Father. Suffering the horrible injury of sin, we struggle to remember who we are as if we have spiritual amnesia. We stumble through life dazed and confused trying to recall where we came from and why we are here. We read a story, our story, and hear of a great fellowship that existed in ancient days. We hear of a Father whose love is fierce, jealous, and redeeming, and we allow our heart to dream, but all we ever find is fool's gold... until we stumble upon the treasure of the Cross and discover the impossible truth: we are not an ugly duckling after all: we are the children of God, and not only does our Father still love us, but He has also been planning for our return.

"But because of his great love for us, God, who is rich in mercy, made us alive with Christ even when we were dead in transgressions — it is by grace you have been saved. And God raised us up with Christ and seated us with him in the heavenly realms in Christ Jesus, in order that in the coming ages

he might show the incomparable riches of his grace, expressed in his kindness to us in Christ Jesus. For it is by grace you have been saved, through faith — and this not from yourselves, it is the gift of God — not by works, so that no one can boast. For we are God's workmanship, created in Christ Jesus to do good works, which God prepared in advance for us to do."

Ephesians 2:4-9

And there, at the Cross, the Spirit of God restores our identity and offers the very things we have been searching for in the sub-consciousness of our heart. The ring is placed on our finger, a feast is prepared, and fellowship is restored as we are given true purpose for our lives and as we learn that we have been saved for a divine task, for work that is sacred. Empowered by the love of the Father, we are equipped for the glory set before us, and ironically, it is this task that will fully transform our hearts, this task that will teach us how to love.

"Dear friends, let us love one another, for love comes from God. Everyone who loves has been born of God and knows God. Whoever does not love does not know God, because God is love. This is how God showed his love among us: He sent his one and only Son into the world that we might live through him. This is love: not that we loved God, but he loved us and sent his Son as an atoning sacrifice for our sins."

1 John 4:7-10

If God is love, then I would say it is impossible to love someone without God. This would imply there are several imitation versions of love out there; meaning that a lot of what we have called love, or thought of as love, was probably not really love at all. We have

139

taken the name of the Lord in vain and we have taken the name of love in vain as well. How can we love if we are not connected to God who is love? If we are going to love, we need God. And this is why: God's love, when fully received through faith in Christ, quenches our thirst for affirmation and converts the once needy heart into a giving heart. A giving heart is necessary for real love. And again, the sacred work of loving others transforms us back into the image of our Father.

"...but whoever drinks the water I give him will never thirst. Indeed, the water I give him will become in him a spring of water welling up to eternal life."   John 4:14

He "whispered" these words to a woman who was thirsty, a woman whose heart had been wounded by five different husbands, a woman who still believed her thirst would be quenched by a man, and lucky for her she finally met the man she was looking for: Jesus. And although we do not have a full record of what He told her, we know this: He quenched her thirst and she indeed became a spring of water welling up to eternal life. The needy heart became a giving heart. Within just a few hours she brought several more people to Jesus who also put their faith in him. She became a spring of living water. She went from looking for love to giving love...and she was fulfilled.

In our own search to quench the passions of our heart, we too climb in bed with some very strange characters. I personally have climbed in bed with material possessions, money, pornography, job

140

status, popularity, etc. We have all had several husbands. And we have all walked away empty. We have all walked away thirsty. And honestly at times I'm not even sure if I really knew what I was looking for in those things. I just knew I was thirsty. And why, after those things almost killed me, did I continue to go back? Why did I "waste my time with repeated futile searches" when I knew they didn't work the first time? Following the world's formula for thirst quenching is like drinking salt water: it will kill you. But luckily for me I also ran into Jesus, and over the years I have been learning more and more about how to drink exclusively from this well of the Father. And through the experience of fellowship with God in ministry I am learning what love is.

"This is love: not that we loved God, but that he loved us and sent his Son as an atoning sacrifice for our sins." 1 John 4:10

Love is humble. Love is gentle. Love is hopeful. Love extends grace. Love overlooks faults. Love moves first. Love persists with kindness. Love endures with hope. Love waits with patience. Love seeks. Love forgives. Love befriends. Love saves. Love redeems. Love "whispers."

Like a child who is loved by his father wants to do what his father does, I have learned that my heart longs not only to be loved, but also *to* love. And because God is love, what better way to learn how to love than to experience God? And it is this new purpose in my life that delivers me from the futility of chasing snipe and fool's gold by creating fellowship with God. If I want to learn how to play basketball, I hang out with Lebron James. If I want to learn how to act, I hang out with Tom Hanks. If I want to learn how to love, I hang out with God. And even my desire to be trained by God's love, my willingness to be transformed in my thinking and values, was inspired by what happened on the Cross. This act of love is the foundation of my trust in God and the root of my affection for my Father. *"We love Him because He first loved us."* The cross is not a fifteen- minute story stuck in the Bible. The cross is the story. All the other stories in the Bible lead to Calvary, they lead to God loving us in Jesus.

"But God demonstrates his own love for us in this: while we were still sinners, Christ died for us."   Romans 5:8

I like the way God asks us to love but shows us how to do it first. And he shows us in a very marvelous way: through the Cross. And you may ask, *"Why does God not pay for our sin himself, why does he not sacrifice himself instead of his own Son?"* Because He loves his Son more than himself. Jesus was the greatest sacrifice God could make and therefore the greatest demonstration of His love. The Cross is the only true way to be loved or to love someone else. If you love someone you will bring them to the Cross. Someone loved me and brought me to the Cross, and it saved my life. (crying)

"If we deliberately keep on sinning after we have received the knowledge of the truth, no sacrifice for sins is left, but only a fearful expectation of

142

judgment and of raging fire that will consume the enemies of God. Anyone who rejected the law of Moses died without mercy on the testimony of two or three witnesses. How much more severely do you think a man deserves to be punished who has trampled the Son of God under foot, who has treated as an unholy thing the blood of the covenant that sanctified him, and who has insulted the Spirit of grace?"

Hebrews 10:26-30

Why would a loving God not appeal to the sinner after death if He truly cares? Because there is no greater appeal than the Cross, there are no words left that might convince, there is no greater persuasion to be offered. When Christ said it was finished, it was truly finished. When Paul wrote about the wrath of God coming on those who reject the Grace of God offered through the Cross, he was saying if this doesn't lead you to repentance and into love with the Father, then nothing can. The separation of non-believers by the justified wrath of God is an act of kindness and protection toward believers. The Cross (the act of Jesus dying for our sins) is the most beautiful and meaningful thing that has ever happened or ever will happen in eternity. It will have no less glory in heaven than on earth. In the book of Revelation, Jesus, the Lamb of God, apparently still displaying his wounds, is front and center. What happened on the Cross can never be trumped or matched. It was the most precious gift that existed, it was the greatest act of love imagined, and it was both God and man's finest moment. The Cross will forever have an impact on believers. When we are walking around heaven and we see the wounded Son of God, it won't be guilt we feel, it will be love, a love that will be newer and stronger with every sunrise, a love that will affirm us with every single breath we take.

143

How can we not believe we are loved in heaven where we have the act of the Cross forever before us, where the wounded Son of God will sit beside us, take our hand into his pierced palm, and say, "*I would do it all over again.*"

The Cross is what connects us to the Father and cures our tendency to go on futile searches. What happened through Jesus and the Cross is so important and so critical to renewing our hearts that we cannot get to the Father unless we go through Jesus. The more connected to Christ and the Cross we become, the more our hearts are transformed by this act of love. The only way to God the Father is through Christ the Son.

"I am the way and the truth and the life. No one comes to the Father except through me. " ... Jesus

Jesus was saying unless we understand God's love displayed through the Cross, we will never be reformed and learn to trust the Father. There is a lie making progress even inside of mainstream Christian circles that says there are many paths to God, but the truth is there can only be many paths to Christ and the Cross. The only thing that can reconcile us to God is the blood of Jesus. The only thing that can save us from our futile searches is the reality of the Cross.

Looking back at my own life I see a pattern of ebb and flow in my relationship with God and not surprisingly in my deep, meaningful relationships with people. I see a pattern of foolishly sipping from the wrong cup. I have had a habit of broken fellowship for too long. It makes no sense to cook a meal you are not going to eat just like it makes no sense to do Christian things but not follow Jesus completely. So many things in life, that require an incredible amount of effort, offer no real satisfaction until they are complete, but once they are complete they redefine the effort as a component of something valuable. Left unfinished, the components are wasted pieces of our time, but completed, the components are the means to a majestic ending. We are not saved by works. We are saved for works, and the work is sacred, meaningful, and life changing. We persevere when we pick up our own cross and follow Him. Our connection to the Cross is what gives us the strength to obey God and take hold of his perfect and good will for our life. We lack commitment because we lack love for God. We lack love for God because we lack a full knowledge of Calvary.

So, will we be changed by the Cross? Will we continue to live the lie or live the truth? Will we finally surrender to God's will for our life or a dangerous mix of our will and a sprinkle of religion? One is a recipe for fulfillment and the other is a recipe for disaster.

In the original story of the Ugly Duckling written in 1844, a duckling endures tremendous taunting and torture because of its odd appearance. The duckling, in search of acceptance, travels to many places looking for safety and love only to suffer rejection and more torture. Eventually, with his spirit crushed, he makes a crucial decision to approach the most majestic birds of all because he believes dying at their hand would be better than the alternative of anything else. But to his surprise, it is here he is freed from his suffering. And so it is for us at the Cross. We fear life with God, we fear what it might require, we fear how we cannot possibly ever change, yet we are not crushed. We are embraced. And in our ear the words *"You are mine"* are whispered and the healing begins.

From the Ugly Duckling
By: Hans Christian Andersen

"I will fly to those royal birds," he exclaimed, "and they will kill me, because I am so ugly, and dare to approach them; but it does not matter: better be killed by them than pecked by the ducks, beaten by the hens, pushed about by the maiden who feeds the poultry, or starved with hunger in the winter."

Then he flew to the water, and swam towards the beautiful swans. The moment they espied the stranger, they rushed to meet him with outstretched wings. "Kill me," said the poor bird; and he bent his head down to the surface of the water, and awaited death. But what did he see in the clear stream below? His own image; no longer a dark, gray bird, ugly and disagreeable to look at, but a graceful and beautiful swan.

To be born in a duck's nest, in a farmyard, is of no consequence to a bird, if it is hatched from a swan's egg. He now felt glad at having suffered sorrow and trouble, because it enabled him to enjoy so much better all the pleasure and happiness around him; for the great swans swam round the new-comer, and stroked his neck with their beaks, as a welcome.

Into the garden presently came some little children, and threw bread and cake into the water.

"See," cried the youngest, "there is a new one;" and the rest were delighted, and ran to their father and mother, dancing and clapping their hands, and shouting joyously, "There is another swan come; a new one has arrived."

Then they threw more bread and cake into the water, and said, "The new one is the most beautiful of all; he is so young and pretty." And the old swans bowed their heads before him.

Then he felt quite ashamed, and hid his head under his wing; for he did not know what to do, he was so happy, and yet not at all proud. He had been persecuted and despised for his ugliness, and now he heard them say he was the most beautiful of all the birds. Even the elder-tree bent down its bows into the water before him, and the sun shone warm and bright. Then he rustled his feathers, curved his slender neck, and cried joyfully, from the depths of his heart, "I never dreamed of such happiness as this, while I was an ugly duckling."

And I weep with you beneath the Cross my friend. But not for long, because bread and cake await, bread and cake await.

"Ashamed of his monstrous form, the beast concealed himself inside his castle, with a magic mirror as his only window to the outside world. The rose she had offered was truly an enchanted rose, which would bloom until his 21st year. If he could learn to love another, and earn her love in return by the time the last petal fell, then the spell would be broken. If not, he would be doomed to remain a beast for all time. As the years passed, he fell into despair and lost all hope. For who could ever learn to love a beast?"
....from the movie *Beauty and the Beast*

BREAD AND CAKE

"I am the bread of life. Your ancestors ate the manna in the wilderness, yet they died. But here is the bread that comes down from heaven, which anyone may eat and not die. I am the living bread that came down from heaven. Whoever eats this bread will live forever. This bread is my flesh, which I will give for the life of the world." ....Jesus

I had a wonderful Grandmother named Flossie who simply lived her life in pink- pink housecoats, pink slippers, pink pants, pink blouses, etc. She loved pink, and she was a bread maker. Flossie had this incredible recipe for hand made yeast bread that was a million years old and must have had Moses's stamp of approval. When she came to visit I remember her telling me, *"Now Timmy, don't poke the dough. It has to rise!"* Of course you know I really wanted to poke the dough after she said that. Half the fun of a balloon is popping it. Ok, ALL the fun of a balloon is popping it. So what possessed me not to poke that dough is beyond me. Maybe if I knew I could eventually eat a balloon I wouldn't pop it either? Anyway, after letting it rise, I also recall how she always pinched off a piece to seed the next batch of dough with the active yeast before she put it in the oven to bake. And the smell...well, let's just say I wanted to sleep on a warm bread pillow.

So the first time I heard Jesus say he was bread I imagined him as a warm, soft, pink, kind of guy that smelled really good. And even the part about eating his flesh sounded good to me. As a kid, I really wanted to take a bite out of Jesus. Even my earliest memories of communion reinforced the idea that Jesus tasted good. I had no idea just how good he really tasted.

King David said, *"Taste the Lord and see that He is good!"* One of my pet peeves is people who say they don't like a particular food but have never even tried it. Another pet peeve is people who believe everything that is healthy must taste bad just like a lot of people believe that God may be a good thing but his instructions are nasty. We treat God like medicine. One of the greatest challenges set before the church today is to deliver the correct, authentic recipe of what it means to have fellowship with God. The true, living God is quite frankly, irresistible and extremely satisfying. There is a dangerous recipe of world mixed with religion being presented as God today, and when this generic religion is ingested it will literally make you spiritually sick. A lot of people are disgusted with their faith, or even God, because their recipe of fellowship is missing key ingredients. We leave out things we determine are not critical, or too difficult to obtain, and then we expect it to still work. We forsake the hard spiritual disciplines of accountability, discipleship, tithing, servanthood, Bible study, etc. because we want an instant easy recipe. Leave the egg and sugar out of the cake and watch what

149

happens. Although love and grace are instantly received, spiritual maturity is a process that comes from submitting our lives to the spiritual disciplines of the Word of God. There are no short cuts. The Word of God not only reveals the true character of God, his authentic values, and overwhelming attractive personality, but it also reveals the path to transformation into the image of His Son. The Word of God sets us free from the lies and reveals to our hearts that God is good and loving. Jesus himself was adamant about setting the record straight about who his Father was. He even said, *"I have come to testify to the truth."* The character of God has been under attack ever since the Garden. Most people don't love God because they are confused about who He is. And the only way to know God is to first accept His true and living bread from Heaven, his one and only begotten Son who expresses his true, good, and loving heart for his children.

Manna was special bread the Israelites were familiar with because it temporarily saved their ancestor's lives during their trek out of Egypt. The distance was 211 miles. It took them 40 years. They averaged 25 yards per day! If you ever thought your progress in Christian maturity was slow, remember the Israelites. They had been in a foreign land for years and you can take the Israelite out of the foreign land, but it takes years to take the foreign land out of the Israelites. During these years of refinement, God reestablished himself as Provider by supplying them with daily bread to keep them physically alive. This special bread fell like dew on the ground every morning for them to gather and eat later in the day. Think about this: God providing bread that saves our life, and keeps us nourished until we reach the Promised Land. Jesus said, "*I am the bread of life.*"

The last day of their enslavement before Pharaoh released them from captivity, an event called the Passover took place. During this event the Israelites were instructed by God to mark their doorpost with the blood of a lamb as a proclamation of their faith in God's deliverance. With blood on their doorframe, the family was spared the last plague of the death angel taking their firstborn son. They were "passed over." The instructions also included that they would eat the meat of the lamb during the night. When Jesus said we must drink his blood and eat his flesh, He was referencing the fact that He was the Lamb of God who was, ironically, sacrificed on the day of Passover.

God doesn't hate sin just because we aren't doing what He told us to do. He hates sin because it harms his children. Sin is contrary to the heart of the One who creates because it destroys what is created. And the reason sin has such dreadful consequences is to protect us from being deceived about it's ability to destroy. Think about how pain is a good thing. The pain in your hand let's you know it is on the stove. The pain in your eye let's you know it has a bug in it scratching your retina. Pain tells us to move our hand and remove the bug. The consequences of sin create an awareness of our Fallen state. So through the curse God creates an environment that is conducive to us becoming aware of the reality of our lostness and sickness. The only thing worse than being lost and sick is being both but not being aware of either. We need help, and this is why we have a Savior. This is why the Bread of Life and Lamb of God came.

And the Bread of Life says there will be dessert in heaven; or in other words we are not only rescued but we are celebrated in the Kingdom of God. There are many mentions of a feast being prepared when a child repents and is found in Christ accepting the forgiveness of God that comes through the sacrifice of His Lamb. The best story is the parable spoken by Jesus about the prodigal son whose misunderstanding of his Father's heart has led him to believe he will be lucky to feed the pigs when he returns home and repents. Instead He finds his father waiting, with open arms, and as he begins to beg for a job, his father interrupts with celebration and welcomes him home by placing a robe on his back and a ring on his finger...and he calls him son. God's greatest mission is the redemption of his children, and his greatest joy is when they return.

In 1981, Jaycee Dugard was kidnapped from her front lawn at the age of eleven. Her stepfather witnessed the abduction and actually tried to chase the kidnappers on a bicycle. For the next 18 years, Jaycee's parents searched for their missing daughter, until 1999 when she was found alive being held captive by her kidnappers. She had been sexually and mentally abused for eighteen years. She had two children of her own fathered by her kidnapper. How do you think Jaycee's parents felt about her dramatic return? How do you think God feels when his children who have been abducted and abused by the Enemy return safely home? No wonder He celebrates.

Birthdays were a pretty big event when I was growing up. We had a $15 budget. I usually asked for a plastic tackle box and a

Zebco 33. I also got to choose a flavor for a cake. I always asked for lemon with lemon frosting. It was a simple pan-cake with about a quarter inch of smooth, creamy, delicious frosting. In a way, I like to think Heaven smelled like lemons the day I turned toward my Father. When I learned that God could love this Beast because He could see my Beauty, it led to my repentance. When I repented and returned to my Father a great celebration broke out with rejoicing in the Kingdom. I remember falling on my knees and begging God to forgive me, praying that I might somehow just squeeze through the door of Heaven and feed the pigs but I underestimated my Father's heart. I wonder if on that day, Heaven filled with the smell of lemon cake and my name was engraved on a gold Zebco 33. And perhaps while He prepared a room for me with a warm bread pillow, the other Saints joined my beloved, pink Flossie in cheering me on toward completing this great, sacred race now set before me.

"Therefore, since we are surrounded by such a great cloud of witnesses, let us throw off everything that hinders and the sin that so easily entangles, and let us run with perseverance the race marked out for us. Let us fix our eyes on Jesus, the author and perfector of our faith, who for the joy set before him endured the cross, scorning its shame, and sat down at the right hand of the throne of God. Consider him who endured such opposition from sinful men, so that you will not grow weary and lose heart. In your struggle against sin, you have not yet resisted to the point of shedding your blood. And you have forgotten that word of encouragement that addresses you as sons:

'My son, do not make light of the Lord's discipline,

and do not lose heart when he rebukes you,

because the Lord disciplines those he loves,

and he punishes everyone he accepts as a son.'

Endure hardship as discipline; God is treating you as sons. For what son is not disciplined by his father? If you are not disciplined (and everyone undergoes discipline), then you are illegitimate children and not true sons. Moreover, we have all had human fathers who disciplined us and we respected them for it. How much more should we submit to the Father of our spirits and live! Our fathers disciplined us for a little while as they thought best; but God disciplines us for our good, that we may share in his holiness. No discipline seems pleasant at the time, but painful. Later on, however, it produces a harvest of righteousness and peace for those who have been trained by it. Therefore, strengthen your feeble arms and weak knees. 'Make level paths for your feet,' so that the lame may not be disabled, but rather healed. "...Hebrews 12

"No true fiasco ever began as a quest for mere adequacy. A motto of the British Special Air Force is: 'Those who risk, win.' A single green vine shoot is able to grow through cement. The Pacific Northwestern salmon beats itself bloody on its quest to travel hundreds of miles upstream against the current, with a single purpose, sex of course, but also... life."

... from the movie Elizabethtown

THE FELLOWSHIP OF SUFFERING

In the movie *Elizabethtown*, a young but successful executive designer of a shoe company makes a fatal mistake that ends up costing his company millions of dollars. He is fired, and later, as he is contemplating suicide by taping a butcher knife to an exercise machine to repeatedly stab himself, he receives news that his father has passed away. He temporarily delays his suicide plan and embarks on a mission to give his father a proper burial. During his trip home he meets an airline stewardess who begins to challenge his pessimistic outlook on life. Several long conversations follow, and eventually, they spend some time together. Over the course of a few days, they fall in love, and the young man begins to catalog the events of his life realizing that his mistakes are not the end but merely part of the process of moving forward toward something more meaningful.

The quote about salmon swimming upstream comes at the end of the film, and I still remember sitting in my living room pondering how profound it was. It was by far one of the best endings to a film I had ever seen. The quote is spoken over the backdrop of several connected video clips. The clip with the fish shows thousands of red salmon in the fight of their life swimming upstream, all crowded into a very narrow piece of water, sacrificing all for the single purpose of preserving their species by mating. I remember rewinding this clip several times and each time feeling like I was understanding something about my life I had never understood before.

Like salmon, I sometimes see myself as one of millions. At times, I feel insignificant, almost invisible in the blend. And sometimes, if not often, it feels like I am swimming upstream, in a very narrow piece of water, in the fight of my life. But what would it mean to me if that swim, my swim, had a purpose? What would it mean to me if I knew what I am doing is an intricate part of preserving the faith, a vital piece in the bigger picture of God's plan for the world? What if this journey upstream jumping waterfalls and dodging grizzlies had two purposes: the continuation of life (a remnant of believers) and the preservation of the spirit of adventure (aka fellowship with God)? And what if this gift of purpose, this call to preservation, this adventure upstream on behalf of my Christian brothers and sisters, was not only my duty, but ironically, also my own path to true fulfillment.

The radical idea of thinking about our individual life in terms of how it helps the people around us is not popular. We live in a society that values the idea of individual celebrity rather than the ideology of commitment to community. Society today idolizes the individual who is popular for contributions that do little to improve the larger community. Sometimes these celebrities even do things that are destructive, but society still clamors to follow them with interest. At some point, I too fell victim to this misdirected search and invested a lot of effort into being individually celebrated because I was misled to believe that popularity is the full potential of a person. But then, over time, I took a close look at the celebrities in the headlines. I didn't see fulfilled, happy people. With a few exceptions, I primarily saw miserable people who make bad decisions. It appeared, from a scientific point of view, that popularity was almost counterproductive to fulfillment. And these sad, popular people are our heroes. And this is what is wrong with us. We have replaced God the Father with American Idols and in effect we are following the wrong leader.

The only people who are worth admiring are those whose life of tireless and humble service has inspired others to follow in their footsteps of sacrificing for the greater good of those around them. While a clown juggling corn may keep us entertained, it is the farmer who keeps us alive. I believe our hearts are geared for an eternal purpose, a purpose that is dual in its nature, a purpose that, beyond all belief, allows us to impact Heaven through our service, and a purpose that prepares our heart for our arrival before our King. The truly great leaders, often unknown people, are those who quietly invest in the idea of building a community through humble service devoted to God and show how, by doing this, they found fulfillment and meaning for their lives. I have an idea that Heaven is going to be full of a lot of people we have never heard of, full of people who quietly and relentlessly loved the Kingdom forward; people, who, like Jesus, helped the sick, aided the poor, washed feet, and picked up their cross; people who understood the fundamental truth that their life was intricately connected to all of mankind and ultimately directed by God the Father; people who swam upstream for a purpose, who lived for a purpose, and even died for a purpose.

The Three Musketeers said, "*One for all and all for one.*" John F Kennedy said, "*Ask not what your country can do for you but ask what you can do for your country.*" But Jesus made the idea a little more compelling when he said, "*The first shall be last and the last shall be first.*" Jesus said if we want to save our life we must first lose it, or once we come to knowledge of the truth there needs to be a radical change in our mentality toward greatness. He even said that if we want to be great we should be a servant. It wasn't a popular idea then and it isn't a popular idea now but it was true then and it is true now. The greatest in the Kingdom of God will be Jesus who "*did not come to be served but rather to serve and give his life as a ransom for many.*" The mind-blowing revelation here is I honestly believe Jesus not only lived as a servant out of obedience but also because it was the most fulfilling and meaningful path to take in life, or servanthood is the best option for living! Most of us think the absence of suffering determines the quality of life but scripture reveals that suffering on behalf of others can be the equivalent of fellowship with God. The Bible is full of radical thoughts and ideas about living life, radical thoughts and ideas that work. Jesus invites us into our true identity and authentic joy when He says, "*Come follow me!*" The Word became flesh and dwelt among us, and the Word is the Way, the Truth, and the Life!

When we elevate our importance and build a tower of ego we not only put the community at risk, but we also sabotage our own fulfillment. Jesus revealed the path to fulfillment comes through serving, through feeding the hungry, taking care of the sick, aiding the poor, and finding the lost. He cast our role as being the light of the world and the salt of the earth. Jesus gave us true purpose.

I remember the first time I heard Max Lucado speak. He spoke for about ten short minutes. He said two things about twenty times, and they meant something to me: *"It is not about you, and it is not about now."* When we grasp the concept that our life is just as much about the lives of the people around us as it is about our own, we begin an incredible journey of faith, a journey that takes us upstream, a journey that beats us against the rocks, a journey that molds our faith, a journey that brings us into fellowship with our Father. And when we are lying there on a rock struggling for air or bleeding in the jaws of a great grizzly, we can say, *"For I am already being poured out like a drink offering, and the time has come for my departure. I have fought the good fight, I have finished the race, I have kept the faith. Now there is in store for me the crown of righteousness, which the Lord, the righteous Judge, will award to me on that day – and not only to me, but also to all who have longed for his appearing. "*

The Apostle Paul also said, *"But whatever was to my profit I now consider loss for the sake of Christ. What is more, I consider everything a loss compared to the surpassing greatness of knowing Christ Jesus my Lord, for whose sake I have lost all things. I consider them rubbish, that I may gain Christ and be found in him, not having a righteousness of my own that comes from the law, but that which is through faith in Christ – the*

159

righteousness that comes from God and is by faith. <u>I want to know Christ</u> *<u>and the power of his resurrection and the fellowship of sharing in his</u>* *<u>sufferings,</u> becoming like him in his death, and so, somehow, to attain to the resurrection from the dead. Not that I have already obtained all this, or have already been made perfect, but I press on to take hold of that for which Christ Jesus took hold of me. Brothers, I do not consider myself yet to have taken hold of it. But one thing I do: Forgetting what is behind and straining toward what is ahead, I press on toward the goal to win the prize for which God has called me heavenward in Christ Jesus. "*

I have spent twenty years in personal, relational ministry with only seven of these as a paid staff person. The other thirteen years I worked a normal job and committed my free time to the pursuit of young people in the name of Christ. I can tell you this: ministry is breathtaking but heartbreaking. During these years of incredible friendships and discipleship, I have also grieved greatly over the suffering of my friends. I have become familiar with the pain of rejection and the almost unbearable burden of loving someone who self-destructs. Although my heart has been hurt and my faith has been challenged, I have also had my mind renewed and my hope emboldened. There were people I love, and still love, who choose not to follow Jesus. There are many still who wrestle with accepting him as both Savior and Lord. Part of their struggle could be connected to my poor leadership, but I also know we both struggle because we share a common Enemy. I have had a front row seat to the consequences of rampant sexual misconduct, the scars and wounds of physical abuse, the damage and destruction of drugs, and even the sting of death by suicide. I have watched my friends suffer.

160

I have watched them bleed. I have watched them cry. I have tried, honestly I have tried, to love these people the best I know how, and yet, the suffering seems endless. It is through this painful process of loving others I have come to know the heart of my Father. I know his heart is broken. I know why his Son wept and I know why his Son had to die... because when you love someone your greatest concern is their suffering and your greatest act of kindness is to become personally acquainted with their suffering to enable your heart for their care and rescue.

Almost everyone has heard the expression, *"walk a mile in my shoes."* It means that to understand people it would be helpful to live as they live, to experience life on their terms. To truly love someone you need to know their story, you need to become familiar with all that has happened to them, you need to know all the pieces of the puzzle to get the big picture. And it is fascinating that God looked down on man and decided to do exactly this, to enter into the human experience.

When we read the New Testament account of the life of Jesus, a few things become very apparent. One, as much as He missed his Father, Jesus appeared to fully enjoy his experience with man in spite of the fact that his visit was heartbreaking. You follow Him through the gospels and you find a Savior whose heart is aware of the crisis of his creation, a Savior who engages the marginalized people of society, a Savior who is actively loving, helping, and serving broken mankind. He is not untouched. He has children on his lap, women clinging to his leg, and men leaning on his shoulder. For four thousand years he has endured the separation of his

161

children created by sin, and now among us again, He embraces the moment. With us, He speaks about the mysteries of God and talks about how man must be born again. With us, He eats and drinks and talks about never thirsting or hungering again. With us, He leads us to repentance referring to us as lost sheep and precious coins. With us, He defends us and loves us by not defending himself as He is hung on a cross. And when it comes time to say good-bye, our Savior once again reaches out to touch us, but this time He washes our feet. (I am crying) The Creator washed the creation's feet.

Two, He intentionally limited his power to familiarize himself with our human sufferings. He did this to prepare himself to become not only a sacrifice for our sin, but also the perfect high priest, our advocate before God. This is the equivalent of me playing Frisbee golf left-handed with my friends. I am very good at throwing a Frisbee but I restrain my power to level the playing field, to make our fellowship more interesting and prevent resentment toward my ability, and, to demonstrate my heart toward them. More than demonstrating his power, Jesus was intent on demonstrating his love. By practicing restraint of his power, He developed an intimate rapport with the disciples. I once heard that the fullness of God is a beautiful, equally fearful, thing to behold. The disguise of his humanness allowed him to slowly reveal himself at a rate that his followers could receive it. Also by subjecting himself to our trials and tribulations, He acquired a unique perspective of our suffering and we acquired a unique perspective of how He responds to it. Jesus has a unique connection to mankind because He endured the fallen human experience, and He has a unique connection to God because he is His only Son. Who then is

162

better to reconcile us to God within the act of the Cross? As He slowly revealed the heart of God over the course of his life, He was preparing our hearts for the unimaginable and unfathomable beauty and horror of Calvary, where no man can stand and every knee shall bow as we look at the full glory of Love.

"During the days of Jesus' life on earth, he offered up prayers and petitions with loud cries and tears to the one who could save him from death, and he was heard because of his reverent submission. Although he was a son, he learned obedience from what he suffered and, once made perfect, he became the source of eternal salvation for all who obey him."

Hebrews 5:7-9

Jesus entered into our suffering to reveal God's love toward us, and He also came to show us how powerful the relationship can be when we love God back. And if we are to love God wouldn't it be helpful to walk a mile in His shoes like He did in ours. Through ministry we enter the heart of God.

Let's take a moment and imagine we have a son, and it is Christmas. We have been busy all morning preparing a huge meal and putting special gifts under the tree. We cannot wait for him to come visit. It has been many years. We miss him dearly. We love him and think about him all the time. Instead he has chosen not to come home. Rather than returning to our outstretched arms he has chosen to rape, torture, and kill a young boy and then dismember the body. Our son is Jeffery Dahmer. Jeffery Dahmer tortured, raped, and dismembered seventeen male victims during his lifetime.

163

His victim's bodies, and body parts, were found hidden in barrels, freezers, shallow graves, and closets. I seriously doubt when his parents held their infant son in their arms they ever imagined the horror that he would grow up to be a serial killer. Nor can I imagine the pain of discovering the details of how their son had thrown his life away and the horrific pain he had created for so many families in the process. Jeffery's father actually reached out to him after he was incarcerated for his crimes and mailed him literature about the Gospel, signifying his broken heart and hope for his son. Neither his mother nor father ever recanted their love for their son, a son the world hated. He was bludgeoned to death by inmates with broomsticks after a few years in prison. Several families of his victims made it publicly known that they approved of his murder. Imagine how it would feel to watch a son you love become something that is so evil that people rejoice at news of his death. God knows how Jeffery Dahmer's parents felt. He watches his children throw their lives away every day. And these are children He loves deeply. He watches them cheat their fathers, kill their brothers, prostitute their sisters, rape their mothers, lie to their neighbors, spit on their Redeemer, rip the flesh off of their Savior, and crucify their King. Yet He comes to us in our prison of sin, and we reach through the bars and we choke Him. (I am weeping) Now you know how God feels. God's heart is broken.

When we devote ourselves to the fellowship of ministry we get acquainted with the grief and suffering of God. As we stand in the gap with our patient, powerful Father and experience the sweat and blood of actively participating in the redemption of his creation we cannot help but love the heart of God even more. I have a deep respect for God, and I must tell you, I cannot imagine how much I, myself, have made God suffer. I am prone to wander. I am a rebellious Son. Grace, grace, amazing grace! I must commit to true repentance that I might bring my Father joy in the midst of this unbearable sea of sin and sadness.

A good friend of mine Kevin Frazier always said, "*Ministry is essentially about sharing the Gospel with the lost, but fundamentally it is about drawing closer to our Father through Jesus.*" The call of ministry is to all of God's children. It is not limited to the missionary in Africa or the minister who leads the church. It is for all of us who confess our sins and profess our love for God. Ministry is the vehicle God uses to synchronize the hearts of men to himself after He saves them through his Son and as He conforms them through his Word. And all of this process is called redemption.

"*Therefore, I urge you, brothers, in view of God's mercy, to offer your bodies as living sacrifices, holy and pleasing to God – this is your spiritual act of worship. Do not conform any longer to the pattern of this world, but be transformed by the renewing of your mind. Then you will be able to test and approve what God's will is – his good, pleasing and perfect will.*"

Romans 12:1-2

When I was a child I was often short on cash, cash needed for candy. The store was a couple of miles from home down a couple of country roads. I would often start walking to the store inspired by my sweet tooth with my pockets empty. As I walked I looked in the ditches and found discarded glass bottles that could be redeemed for ten or even twenty-five cents. The bottles were usually filled with brown waste-water and covered in mud. I would hand the bottles to the store clerk and they would hand me my money. The bottles were then picked up a few days later by the vendor and returned to the factory where they were washed, sanitized, and refilled with soda as they were created to be. This is how redemption works.

Our problem is many of us have been found and maybe even surrendered to the cleaning process, but very few have been sanitized by the Word and refilled with the true transforming purpose of ministering to others. Not only is it sad that we are missing fulfillment but it is also sad that we fail to discover the true heart of God. Our churches are full of empty bottles; our churches are full of sad people who do not know the heart of their Father and who do not trust his Word.

And it is here we come to a great revelation: we are filled to assist the thirst of others. When people drink from our well, is the water bitter or sweet? Our relationships with people suffer because our relationship with God suffers. And it especially difficult when we are labeled as sweet and refreshing but our hearts are empty and bitter. Our fellowship with God must be restored if our fellowship with others is to be restored.

"Therefore, if anyone is in Christ, the new creation has come; the old has gone, the new is here! All this is from God, who reconciled us to himself through Christ and gave us the ministry of reconciliation: that God was reconciling the world to himself in Christ, not counting people's sins against them. And he has committed to us the message of reconciliation. We are therefore Christ's ambassadors, as though God were making his appeal through us. We implore you on Christ's behalf: Be reconciled to God. God made him who had no sin to be sin for us, so that in him we might become the righteousness of God."

2 Corinthians 5:17-21

166

"If you have any encouragement from being united with Christ, if any comfort from his love, if any fellowship with the Spirit, if any tenderness and compassion, then make my joy complete by being like-minded, having the same love, being one in spirit and purpose. Do nothing out of selfish ambition or vain conceit, but in humility consider others better than yourselves. Each of you should look not only to your own interests, but also to the interests of others. Your attitude should be the same as that of Christ Jesus: Who, being in the very nature of God did not consider equality with God something to be grasped, but made himself nothing, taking the very nature of a servant, being made in human likeness. And being found in appearance as a man, he humbled himself and became obedient to death — even death on a cross!"

Philippians 2:1-8

There is a show I love to watch called *Extreme Home Makeover*. The show simply reaches out to families suffering a hardship complicated by their living conditions. The show's hosts surprise the family and ship them off on a fantastic vacation while, in the course of a week, they build them the home of their dreams. I cry every time I watch the show. Now, let's imagine the family thinks about how difficult it will be to pack a few things, part with old memories, and change their schedule to accommodate the makeover. Let's say they think about it and say no thanks because they hate change. Are they tired of living they way they do? Yes! But they refuse to change. Crazy, isn't it? Welcome to the life of most Christians.

God tells us to pack our clothes, to say our good-byes, and to undergo a process of change because He wants to give us an extreme makeover. He tells us to trust Him and it will be the best thing that

167

has ever happened to us. The limousine that pulls up happens to be a red limousine of ministry (it is a huge privilege to do the work of God). We say no thanks because we don't like the color red. We'd rather continue the insanity of pursuing fellowship on our own terms, terms that have failed in the past. If only we could see behind the bus, if only we could see the plan God has for us, a plan to prosper us and not to harm us. If only we would trust the leadership of God in scripture and experience the joy that comes from joining him in the fellowship of temporary suffering so that one day we might stand with our brothers and sisters of the faith and with a fist pump scream, "MOVE THAT BUS," as we fall to our knees from awe when our Father's heart is revealed to those who know him.

"But we have this treasure in jars of clay to show that this all-surpassing power is from God and not from us. We are hard pressed on every side, but not crushed; perplexed, but not in despair; persecuted, but not abandoned; struck down, but not destroyed. We always carry around in our body the death of Jesus, so that the life of Jesus may also be revealed in our body."

2 Corinthians 4:7-10

"Therefore we do not lose heart. Though outwardly we are wasting away, yet inwardly we are being renewed day by day. For our light and momentary troubles are achieving for us an eternal glory that far outweighs them all. So we fix our eyes not on what is seen, but on what is unseen. For what is seen is temporary, but what is unseen is eternal."

2 Corinthians 4:16-18

"Jesus said no greater love hath any man than that a man would lay down his life for his friends. He called us friends and then He died and loved us."

LOVE LOVES

When I started out on this journey I wanted to improve the quality of the relationships in my life. I wanted to make sure that when it came time for me to die to make certain that not only had I lived, but even more so, that I had actually really loved.

"This is love: not that we loved God, but that he loved us and sent his Son as an atoning sacrifice for our sins"   1 John 4:10

A simple truth that continues to resonate in my heart is that my understanding of God's love for me enables my love for others. Until I fully experience grace, I cannot understand the fundamental principles of love. Me trying to love someone apart from God's grace is like a caterpillar trying to fly out of the top of a tree with no wings. Although the capacity to love is in me, it remains ultimately unlocked, or restrained, until it is released in my heart by my coming to terms with how both desperate and blessed I am for God's sacrifice for my sin that has grieved his own heart. My humble, thankful heart is fertile ground for love.

I once tweeted I have the eyes of David, the mouth of Moses, the mind of Peter, and the heart of Judas, but I am forgiven. I am well acquainted with my sin and my weaknesses. I am equally aware of the price that was paid for my redemption. This awareness creates in me both a deep sense of gratitude toward God and a compassionate understanding for others who are sick and lost. I can identify with their pain, but I do not condone sin. And I do not believe Christians should continue to regularly sin. For one, it grieves the heart of God; two, it hurts others; and three, it hurts us. The reason Christians struggle so much with sin is because we don't grasp what our sin costs nor do we grasp the depths of the love that is willing to pay the ransom. The more we understand the love of God the less we sin. The more we understand the cost of our own rescue the more compassion we have for those who are still lost.

My own battle with sin as a believer is something I am willing to share. I believe sin is a roadblock to love. Sin interrupts fellowship by distracting the heart with concealment rather than intimacy.

My biggest struggle has been lust, which I documented in a very transparent way in my first book Chainsaw Preacher: A True Story. After several years of suffering from pornography, I have made tremendous strides in reducing its frequency but recently realized my environment was not totally conducive to bringing it fully under control. I realized that I needed to make radical changes in my music, television, and internet choices. I needed to create an environment conducive to my spiritual obedience (safety). I've learned to look at godly discipline as setting myself up to succeed in relationships rather than simply jumping through hoops to hear the applause of God. He isn't interested in training me for a circus. He is interested in training me to become a healthy child.

A great way to look at occasional sin is to think about it like we are pouring a few drops of poison on our flowers once a year. It may not kill them, but they certainly won't grow like they are supposed to. And why, if we can get rid of it, do we keep the poison on the shelf? Like, why keep certain media in my life if it has the potential to trigger a severe reaction? We need to set ourselves up to win, to love, and to be loved. We need to create safe environments for ourselves that are conducive to our spiritual and relational health.

And in setting up this environment, as we conduct our spring cleaning, we also need to add some things to fertilize our heart, simple things like: Bible study, prayer, church fellowship, mentorship, volunteer service, etc. These interactions with truth help erase the lies sown in our heart by Satan. Sanctification (cleaning) with truth needs to be a regular component of our lives. We need a renewing of our mind, and this will not happen without exposure to the teaching and learning of God's word. We must replace the lies with the truth.

The next thing we need to do is eliminate stress in our life by conducting our business and personal lives according to God's instructions, to become doers of the word and not hearers only. By being organized, punctual, diligent, and respectful workers and employers we protect our testimony and we eliminate stress caused by disorganization, missed opportunities, and pressure from the burden of unfinished projects and broken promises. Stress creates a weakness in our spirit that becomes a target for sin to take a foothold. A tiny crack in the foundation of a building can compromise the entire structure over time. Water can collect in the crack, freeze, and bust the foundation. Satan attacks our areas of stress. It is wise to eliminate the opportunity for sin to disrupt our fellowship by conducting ourselves in a way that minimizes the potential to damage our testimony to others who are watching.

"Be wise in the way you act toward outsiders; make the most of every opportunity. Let your conversation be always full of grace, seasoned with salt, so that you may know how to answer everyone."

Colossians 4:5-6

Perhaps the biggest problem facing Christians today is the baggage of concealed sin. We hide our sin from each other because we are embarrassed. It is very difficult to rationalize how we can hide sin from an all-seeing God, so instead we try to hide God. We put Him as far out of our mind as we can, so we don't have to think about grieving his heart. Sadly, we suffer from the burden of sin even though the Word of God is very clear on presenting an effective system for avoiding the pitfall of guilt. It is called confession. Most Christians don't use this critical ingredient of spiritual discipline in their lives and thus suffer the absence of meaningful fellowship within the body. Concealed sin destroys fellowship by tainting our spirit within our relationships. We adopt the mentality of *"Oh well I already messed up so why keep trying."* Or, the guilt creates a point of stress weakening our resolve to resist temptation. Christians with unconfessed sin are like athletes with a pulled muscle trying to compete in the Olympics. Not only does confession bring healing, but it also strengthens bonds within community. Honesty and

172

transparency are conducive to intimacy. Read that twice. Honesty and transparency are conducive to intimacy. Accountability guards the heart from sin to protect the seeds of love. Without weekly or even daily accountability we rob ourselves of healthy relationships.

"Therefore confess your sins to each other and pray for each other so that you may be healed. The prayer of a righteous man is powerful and effective."
James 5:16

The Bible says that love lasts forever. A part of me wants to insert the word *true* love lasts forever into that statement to explain why many of my attempts at love failed. But I have learned that much of what I called love in my life wasn't love at all. Much of what I called loving others was me selfishly pursuing allies to serve my needs. My definition of love was more about what I could get than what I could give. I've since learned the love of God is complete in giving me what I need; thus, I am free to focus on others. I believe there is a great need to salvage the definition of true love from the wreckage of bad information that has created so much collateral damage in our world today.

To understand our need for a real definition, we need to look at the problem. Consider four people sitting at a square table. Each one has a piece of paper upon which they privately write down what they think it means to love someone. Upon examination, we would discover their definitions vary and are actually quite different. And thus we have a problem don't we? The problem is that when someone at the table says they love someone else at the table they mean what they wrote on their paper, but the person who has been told they are loved believes they actually mean what is on their paper! Because we all have a different understanding of what love means, we run the risk of having false expectations and getting hurt by what we believe are broken promises and sometimes empty words. So we see how there is a need for a universal definition of love, and the Bible does not leave us hanging.

First, the Bible reveals that God is love, or all the attributes of love are displayed in God's eternal character. Second, the Bible gives us a demonstration of love in Jesus. And this isn't just a demonstration of God's love toward us, but also a demonstration of how we are supposed to love one another. Jesus said, *"Love one another as I have loved you."* He said the greatest commandment is to first love God and second is to love our neighbor as ourself. Jesus said there is no greater love than us learning to lay down our lives for our friends. He said these two loves summed up all the other commandments. And what are commandments to the believer? They are stepping stones toward true fellowship.

Following these stepping-stones doesn't mean we are exempt from suffering or heartache. We live in a free will world that is cursed, a world that is conducive to us discovering our need for God. Christians who identify with God through ministry will not only be heartbroken, but will also struggle with the same components of our fallen world as everyone else will. Cancer and house fires attack believers just like they do nonbelievers. Jesus said we would have trouble, even be persecuted because of our faith, or, our hardship would actually increase because of our association with

Him. So why follow God? What are the benefits? How about true meaningful fellowship in the midst of the chaos, sincere hope for eternal restoration, and a transforming perspective that brings authentic joy in spite of suffering and persecution. If we are going to be underwater either way why not learn how to use a snorkel? I personally crave true meaningful fellowship in the midst of suffering. I enjoy intimate community framed by an urgency for ministry. I desire purpose on the battlefield of life. I want to learn how to love and be loved so my life matters in the sand of time. I want true authentic eternal fellowship.

The Bible emphasizes our need for love by warning us of possessing a hollow heart. It says we can use eloquent words and master compliments but without love our voice is annoying. It says we can know everything about everything, and become an expert on all subjects, but without love, we are useless to the people around us. It even says that we can be fully vested in our planet, even willing to contribute everything we have, but without love we are wasting our time. So I would say it is critical to have love and to understand love, and that without love our life has no meaning.

For me to pretend that I can explain in one chapter what God is like or what love is like would be the same as me saying I can explain <u>Gone With the Wind</u> in four words. In some ways, the Gospel is a cliff note to the broad love of God aided by the powerful, life altering, visual aid of Jesus crucified on a cross. But, even John said if an attempt was made to describe everything about Jesus, the world could not contain the books. Yet, we do have the living, breathing Word of God and it takes the time to explain how we too can love.

"Dear friends, since God so loved us, we also ought to love one another."

1 John 4:11

To love is a command, but a command from God is a flare-gun shot up in the air of chaos to lead us to safety. A command from God is a stepping-stone in the swamp of life. Commandments are the critical roadmaps to successful relationships.

Our greatest need is to be loved by God, and our greatest purpose is to follow God's example of love. And the scripture plainly tells us how the Holy Spirit wants to conform us into the image of his Son.

"Love is patient, love is kind. It does not envy, it does not boast, it is not proud. It does not dishonor others, it is not self-seeking, it is not easily angered, it keeps no record of wrongs. Love does not delight in evil but rejoices with the truth. It always protects, always trusts, always hopes, always perseveres."

1 Corinthians 13

Now let's substitute the name God for love because the scripture tells us God is love.

God is patient, God is kind. God does not envy, God does not boast, God is not proud. God does not dishonor others, God is not self-seeking, God is not easily angered, God keeps no record of wrongs. God does not delight in evil

176

but rejoices with the truth. God always protects, always trusts, always hopes, always perseveres.

Now as we look back at the life of Jesus let us substitute Jesus for love because Jesus said His Father and He are one.

Jesus was patient, Jesus was kind. Jesus did not envy, Jesus did not boast, Jesus was not proud. Jesus did not dishonor others, Jesus was not self-seeking, Jesus was not easily angered, Jesus kept no record of wrongs. Jesus did not delight in evil but rejoiced with the truth. Jesus always protected, always trusted, always hoped, and always persevered.

The haunting question is do we imitate the love of God or an artificial version? When we tell someone we love them, are we saying we will be patient with them; we will be kind to them; we will not view them as competition; we will not let our pride get in the way of meeting their needs; we will not say bad things about them; we will control our emotions; we will forgive and forget; we will not celebrate nor condone their sin but we will encourage them toward godly living; we will protect them; we will trust them; we will always wish them well; and we will be truly committed to them?

There is a great need to replace our working definition of love with truth, and there is an even greater need to replace our mirage of emotional connection with the deep-rooted reality of a love that is God based. It is rather easy to figure out that if we all loved others the way God loves us our relationships would dramatically be transformed. So what holds us back? The me factor: our own bad habits and engrained way of destructive thinking that has taken us hostage. And this is why we need to submit ourselves to the leadership of God through committing ourselves to the study of his instructions, instructions that take us where we want to go, instructions that teach us how to love like He loved, instructions that "free" us from an empty way of life.

If we believe God is good, then wouldn't his commandments and ideas about how to love be good too? It comes down to a matter of trust. Somehow we tend to believe we can invent shortcuts and get where we want to go. We trust ourselves more than God! How can we trust that God can save us from our sins but can't believe He can lead us into meaningful, sustaining relationships? If He can do a heart transplant, don't you think He can make a peanut butter and jelly sandwich? Give God credit!

"For I know the plans I have for you," declares the Lord, "plans to prosper you and not to harm you, plans to give you hope and a future." **Jeremiah 29:11**

"I imagine that right now, you're feeling a bit like Alice. Hmm? Tumbling down the rabbit hole? *You could say that.* I see it in your eyes. You have the look of a man who accepts what he sees because he is expecting to wake up. Ironically, that's not far from the truth. Do you believe in fate, Neo? *No.* Why not? *Because I don't like the idea that I'm not in control of my life.* I know exactly what you mean. Let me tell you why you're here. You're here because you know something. What you know you can't explain, but you feel it. You've felt it your entire life, that there's something wrong with the world. You don't know what it is, but it's there, like a splinter in your mind, driving you mad. It is this feeling that has brought you to me. Do you know what I'm talking about? *The Matrix.* Do you want to know what it is? *Yes.* The Matrix is everywhere. It is all around us. Even now, in this very room. You can see it when you look out your window or when you turn on your television. You can feel it when you go to work... when you go to church... when you pay your taxes. It is the world that has been pulled over your eyes to blind you from the truth. *What truth?* That you are a slave, Neo. Like everyone else you were born into bondage, into a prison that you cannot taste or see or touch, a prison for your mind. I'm trying to free your mind, Neo. But I can only show you the door. You're the one that has to walk through it."   *...from the movie The Matrix*

DON'T BE A DONUT

When I started this book I was living all alone in a hundred year old house with sixteen rooms. Four years ago I swore I'd never live alone. I guess I broke my own promise. A promise I should have kept.

I got lonely every once in awhile, especially when I watched movies like *Seven Pounds*. I walked around drinking glass Dr. Peppers and staring out of one of my 52 windows. I usually circled back to the computer and checked my email for a note from the girl of my dreams but instead found more junkmail about my six million dollar inheritance awaiting me in Africa. I would stumble into the kitchen and watch TV Land while eating a bowl of Raisin Bran. For the most part I stayed busy but these occasional lonely moments were occurring regularly. And then one day it struck me that something about my life was horribly wrong. And as I worked through the issues I figured out what it was: I was evaluating my life with a value system I had determined was flawed. I was creating my own misery.

I imagine most people's lives are full of misery created by their pursuit of, and attachment to, things that are completely worthless. Yet for most people, the misery is somewhat muted by the fact they don't know they are pursuing a dead end. The Christians who continue to pursue and attach themselves to things that are completely worthless are actually the most miserable people of all because they know they are wasting their time.

For me the misery fed itself. Because I was evaluating my life by flawed worldly standards, I derived worthless conclusions about what was needed to fix my problem. I poured huge amounts of time and effort into perfecting my business, landscaping my yard, and methodical house keeping while neglecting my spiritual issues. I was half right. I needed to pursue perfecting something, but it wasn't a hundred year old house, it was a thirty-year old faith.

"The only thing that counts is faith expressing itself through love."

Galatians 5:6

The one thing in my life that counts, I was neglecting. I was taking care of everything else but my faith evolving into radical love, the

180

one part of me that will actually last. I was focusing on things that don't last. I was focusing on the wrong things. I was in bondage to a system I had declared was inaccurate and flawed. Not only was I wasting my time but I was also wasting my life. I was a jelly donut with nothing but air inside.

" As the Father has loved me, so have I loved you. Now remain in my love. If you obey my commands, you will remain in my love, just as I have obeyed my Father's commands and remain in his love. I have told you this so that my joy may be in you and that your joy may be complete. My command is this: Love each other as I have loved you. Greater love has no one than this, that he lay down his life for his friends. You are my friends if you do what I command. I no longer call you servants, because a servant does not know his master's business. Instead, I have called you friends, for everything that I learned from my Father I have made known to you. You did not choose me, but I chose you and appointed you to go and bear fruit—fruit that will last. Then the Father will give you whatever you ask in my name. This is my command: Love each other."

John 15:9-17

Jesus said if we abide in him we will produce fruit, fruit that lasts. And we discover these fruits are love, joy, peace, patience, kindness, goodness, faithfulness, gentleness, and self-control. For most of my life I have been a tree that has struggled with producing fruit. Oh, I had plenty of leaves, and even plenty of height, but I was short in the fruit market. And I have learned that my roots were being impeded by my resolution to have my own way. And I was also in desperate need of a pruning. I honestly believe this is what has been happening to me in the process of writing this book: I have been pruned. And here is what I have learned.

181

Distraction is only defeated with contentment.

Contentment is only gained through deep relationship with God.

Relationship with God grows through obedience.

Obedience grows with the depth of our understanding of God's love.

By committing ourselves to the Word of God we reinforce the truths that we are a child of God and He loves us deeply. The Word of God shifts our focus from the temporary things to the eternal things. It simply reduces the stress related to life by revealing the insignificance of the things that overwhelm us. The Word of God delivers us from an empty way of life freeing us up to pursue the more noble things of God, things that last.

"Rejoice in the Lord always. I will say it again: Rejoice! Let your gentleness be evident to all. The Lord is near. Do not be anxious about anything, but in everything, by prayer and petition, with thanksgiving, present your requests to God. And the peace of God, which transcends all understanding, will guard your hearts and your minds in Christ Jesus. Finally, brothers, whatever is true, whatever is noble, whatever is right, whatever is pure, whatever is lovely, whatever is admirable – if anything is excellent or praiseworthy – think about such things. Whatever you have learned or received or heard from me, or seen in me – put it into practice. And the God of peace will be with you. ....I have learned to be content whatever the circumstances. I know what it is to be in need, and I know what it is to have plenty. I have learned the secret of being content in any and every situation, whether well fed or hungry, whether living in plenty or in want. I can do everything through him who gives me strength."

Philippians 4

I think we do a pretty good job of telling ugly ducklings that they are swans, but we do a horrible job of teaching them what swans do. Swans live different lives than ducks, and swans have a different view of the pond. Our biggest failure in the Christian community today is the lack of true discipleship. We have a problem with commitment to transformative teaching. And one reason we don't disciple people is because we weren't discipled. The lack of infusion of truth into the lives of believers is why we have a relational crisis on our hands. And the reason we don't disciple people is because we don't have the heart for it. Only a godly, patient love can withstand the slow pace of spiritual progress in the lives of most people. We can't feed people with the fruit of the Spirit if we aren't producing fruit. We aren't producing fruit because we are distracted with things that don't matter.

This was as convicting for me as it is for you. I took an honest look at how I spent my time and it scared me. I am convinced how we spend our time is a reflection of what we truly believe. If we believe God is central to life, I would think how we spend our time would reflect that. When I looked at my life I found a lot of things that didn't matter were crowding my top ten. It was frustrating to realize I was distracted, but it was obvious why: I had stopped abiding in the Word and was struggling with the concept of obedience.

I believe most people look at godly discipline with resentment because of our childhood experiences. As a child our parents typically told us to do things we really didn't want to do, things like brush our teeth, eat our vegetables, and clean our room. The thing I hated most about my childhood was I was forced to sleep with a T-shirt on. Could not stand it! Drove me crazy!!! As a matter of fact I would let it hang around my neck to appear as if I had it on while letting the sheets cover my bare chest. My mom would come to give me a good night kiss, rip the covers back, and say, "WHY YOU," and yanked me out of bed while she spanked my cushion! All of these things were meant for my good and literally helped me grow up healthy but at the time, because I lacked wisdom, I resented the instructions. We resent godly discipline because we lack wisdom. As we gain Godly wisdom we appreciate the clarity and safety of God's instruction. We need to wear our t-shirt and trust God.

The goal of discipleship should be to conform us into the image of His Son, Jesus. We surrender to God's leadership because He has proven trustworthy. Discipleship should focus on two things, learning and applying the Word of God. Discipleship should teach us how to love like Jesus. The difficult part of discipleship is being corrected and challenged because we don't like to do things like brush our teeth and eat our vegetables. But He loves us and His words are life. A true friend will not sit on the sidelines and watch us self-destruct. They will speak the truth in love asking us to repent. Remember, love does not delight in evil, but rejoices with the truth.

Once I arranged my environment to coincide with God's plan for my life, I started seeing fruit in my life. It took Bible study, accountability, confession, prayer, tithing, serving, and ministering to get me moving in the right direction. While I had the control to change some things, others things around me remained beyond my control to change. But even with these things, I changed my perspective. My relationships, although not exponentially increasing in number, began to explore new depths of connection and loyalty for the few I focused on. My life was better because my love for God was better, and I only loved Him because He first loved me. My response to God's love determined the quality of my life.

I grew up on a farm and learned very early in life how planting and growing works. You plant your life in the ground of good discipleship and root yourself in the love and Word of God. You water your life with godly fellowship and prune your life with accountability and confession. There will be dry seasons and wet seasons. There will be late frost and summer storms. Your leaves will get burned by blight, and your trunk will be attacked by beetles. But if you stand there year after year and survive nature's fury of sin, if you persevere, beautiful children will come and climb in your branches to taste the fruit of the Lord and see that He is good. There are no shortcuts to bearing fruit that will last, but there is a path. It is narrow and it is straight...but it leads to life, not just for you, but also for all those around you who are desperate for a taste of Love. The leaves of a casual Christian are great, but the hungry lost can starve to death under a shade tree. *"Go and bear fruit, fruit that lasts."*

LOVE LIKE YOU ARE DYING

So here we are at the end. I stand back and look at what I shared and need to ask a question. Are we any different? Are we prepared to go out and love God and love the people around us? Are we ready to live the best life possible, which is an obedient life? Do we know how? Is the path clear? Or, will we settle for the status quo? Will we continue to live the great compromise of a lukewarm religion? Our life depends on what we do. Perhaps there is one last thing I could share that might be helpful. She died last year, but I don't think she would mind me telling you this.

I get asked to do weddings all the time. Typically they are young adults that I ministered to while they were in high school. I've got four weddings this year. They are usually festive, fun events that I really enjoy but on a rare occasion I get another kind of phone call, a phone call to do a funeral. I got one last year. Her name was Tara Stover. She was 28 years old. She was a dear friend of mine. And she ministered to me.

As a child she was diagnosed with cancer, which she beat, but the radiation took its toll on her body. Her fight left her with a multitude of ongoing medical conditions. One of her battle scars was her spine was severely curved and her own body put

186

tremendous stress on her lungs. As they struggled to keep up, Tara was forced to get a permanent trache (a hole or port in her throat). Inserted into this hole was a tube that supplied her weak lungs with pure oxygen. This made it necessary for her to have several pieces of heavy medical equipment that she lugged around to keep her breathing. She was hospitalized several times during her life because of her medical problems. She might have weighed eighty pounds, but she kept fighting back. She graduated college with a master's degree. She got a job. And she even moved out on her own. In spite of her lack of energy and burden of medical equipment, she volunteered her time to help several different organizations in our community. In the summer she devoted two weeks of her time to the same cancer camp, Rising Sun, that she had attended during her own battle with cancer. She was a video expert and would spend hundreds of hours editing and creating great memories on film for campers. For me, she taped and edited several high quality Young Life club videos. And I remember she did all this while dragging around that heavy medical equipment.

One specific thing she did still echoes through my life. She had a pool party. It was obvious she couldn't swim because of her trache, but she had a pool party. She invited several of the people she knew to her parent's backyard and had a pool party. Just so you understand this, she was weak, all the time; it was hard for her to breathe. Yet she was always looking outward, surveying her world, and asking what she could do for others. She put others first.

Tara had a different perspective of life because she knew her time was brief. She had a different view of life because she had been through an incredible process of being loved during her suffering. Doctors, nurses, family, and friends were constantly by her bedside as her struggle unfolded with visits in and out of the hospital. Her heart was a masterpiece painted by the compassion of others and framed beautifully by her small window of time. And I believe her life was complete, finished in its truest sense.

The Bible says our lives are also framed, bound by a small window of time. Our life is like a vapor in the wind, a fading flower, a shadow of the things to come. If we truly believed we are dying, it would change how we live, and it would change how we love. This awareness of our own brevity should not create fear but rather focus. Tara had focus. I think what enables our heart to transcend our fear, and focus on loving others, is experiencing the redemptive love of God. It is the goodness of God that leads men to repentance (true transformational change) just like it was the incredible care Tara received that transformed her into a very caring, focused person. How much we allow God's love to transform us will determine how much we can help transform others. Our time with God, even during suffering, prepares our heart to love others. The most fertile soil is in a floodplain. In high water, we experience His rescue, and, when the water recedes, a heart that has walked through suffering, a heart that has been cradled by God, is a heart that can follow a Chicken Whisperer and love others.

I think sometimes we look at following God the same way we look at the Bible. We see something thick, mysterious, difficult, and optional. We see it that way because we lack the perspective that comes from wisdom. The will of God is clear and simple: He has set out to redeem his children. God wants us in eternity. Our Creator craves his creation's heart's eternal salvation. And that news should fill our hearts with a joyous hope that inspires us to become an active ally in God's redemption of the world through His Son. If we really care about a relationship, if we are focused, we should connect that relationship to God because it will allow that relationship to go with us into eternity.

When Jesus walked on the earth we had the privilege of seeing God's own response to suffering. Jesus said if we have seen him, we have seen his Father. What we discover is God's message of love is always framed in small, practical acts of kindness. He heals the bleeding woman, gives sight to the blind man, and heals the leper's disease. He tells us that it is the small, practical acts of love like a cup of water for a child and a simple visit to the sick that echo through heaven. He says the widow's small offering is actually huge; a small, sincere prayer is preferred over rhetoric; and a small act of faith can rearrange the face of the earth. He doesn't tell us to build buildings, erect statues, or nail up plaques. He tells us to go and defend God's name and nature and to tell the accurate story of God's love for man. And the night before his death, He tells us to love like He loves. He tells us, "*Come follow Me!*"

Are we too scared or too distracted to carry out the Great Commission of God? We have been lulled into believing we are insignificant in the bigger scheme of things, and our presence, or our absence, has no impact on God's plan for redemption. We doubt our potential. We doubt the design and the Designer. And we need to repent. We need to die to our old way of living. Jesus said,

"Verily, verily, I say unto you, Except a corn of wheat fall into the ground and die, it abideth alone: but if it die, it bringeth forth much fruit."

Seeds are deceptive. They have tremendous potential. A seed stopped up my sewage system, a seed cracked my concrete driveway, a seed fell on my house and broke my roof, a seed kept my parents warm all winter, a seed kept Noah dry, a seed cradled Jesus at birth, and a seed became the alter where God's blood was shed. A seed that grew did all those things. When a seed is put in good soil at the right temperature with the right amount of light and the right amount of moisture, it grows, and over time it does something unimaginable: it changes the landscape around it! But it can't do anything unless it is placed in the right conditions. Nor can we. Until we bury our old way of living, submerse ourselves in the Word of God, drink from the love of the Cross, and walk in the light of sincere obedience, nothing will change. But when we do, we change the world and bring forth much fruit.

Forty years ago a seed was planted in my life by a woman named Brenda Knipper. She is a woman who has never married and by all means appears to the world to be quite ordinary. She has always lived her life in reverence to God. She held me in the church nursery when I was just a few weeks old and followed me along as I grew up by teaching various classes throughout my childhood. She was no great speaker, maybe even shy, yet she had a voice that reverberated in my mind with her relentless, practical acts of love toward me.

190

Cookies and kool-aid enticed me to learn the books of the Bible while Pop Rocks bribed me to memorize scripture, but it was her personal example of investment that brought the Word of God to life. There were ten or so of us kids that she poured her life into, and she never asked for praise. We didn't behave, we didn't listen, and we didn't notice at the time we were being tenderly loved in a very godly way by a very godly woman. Although she had a full time job, her whole life's focus was taking excellent care of her elderly mother and familiarizing a loud, sugar obsessed, skinny kid with the Word of God. Her small, practical acts of love took root in my heart and I believe they played a huge role in saving my life. (I am crying)

The Enemy has created a unique way for us to rationalize the slow relational suicide of forsaking God's plan for life, His plan of experiencing love by loving others. In our quest to save our life we have traded the truth of God for a lie, and we have dug a grave of selfishness. Sometimes I believe we realize what we are doing and the destruction we are causing. We realize we are headed in the wrong direction but the hole is just too deep, so we just keep digging. Sometimes we just want to hurry up and die...but then here comes Jesus.

There is one story in scripture I believe speaks to those of us who are struggling with change late in life. It is that of the thief who was crucified along side of Jesus at Calvary.

Jesus, like my friend Tara, knew his life was brief. And this awareness that his death was imminent propelled him to extract every ounce of opportunity out of his time here on earth. His life was defined by his devoted obedience (His love for His father) and his steadfast sacrifice (His love for me and you) framed in practical acts of kindness. John said if he attempted to record all the things Jesus said and did the world could not contain the books. And yet, even as his busy life was coming to a close, as He was staring death in the face, He comforted a thief.

"Then one of the criminals who were hanged blasphemed Him, saying, "If You are the Christ, save Yourself and us." But the other, answering, rebuked him, saying, "Do you not even fear God, seeing you are under the same condemnation? And we indeed justly, for we receive the due reward of our deeds; but this Man has done nothing wrong." Then he said to Jesus, "Lord, remember me when You come into Your kingdom." And Jesus said to him, "Assuredly, I say to you, today you will be with Me in Paradise."

Luke 23:39-43

It is never too late to be changed or help someone change. A thief, whose life was riddled with bad decisions and destroyed by poor choices, admits two things: he was wrong and He is right. Some argue this thief never heard the Gospel, and I agree, he didn't hear it... he saw it. He saw an innocent, powerful Son of God nailed to a Cross, humble himself. He saw the Man who had raised the dead now dying for the people who were crucifying Him. This thief witnessed the greatest act of love in history and it was personalized when Jesus turned to him and spoke comforting words of life while He, himself, was dying. Nailed to a cross, his flesh hanging in strips from his ribs, his eyes stinging from his own blood, struggling to breathe, He saved one more stray sheep. Nearing his last breath when He would say, *"it is finished,"* He was still searching for the lost. He could have just closed his eyes and the thief would still have been saved, but no, our Jesus, our Redeemer, spoke because He knew his words would bring comfort to a thief who was now forgiven. Jesus was weak, it was hard for him to breathe, but He loved, even while He was dying.

And who better to love a dying thief. He was being crucified just like a thief. He was even hated just like a thief. But He put himself in that position, that position of whisperering, of assuming not only a thief's desperate situation but ours as well. And Our Whisperer spoke to all thieves, to all of us who are guilty, to all of us who cry out in our pain, to all of us who have wasted our lives, *"Today you will be with Me in Paradise."* (I am crying)

There are a million excuses and they are all lies. When we forsake God's plan for life, we forsake his love. When we forsake His love, we forsake our most critical need. Now is the time to trust a greater wisdom than our own. And if we think obedience, following God's incredibly clear and direct path for our life, is too hard, let us remember my friend Tara and our Lord Jesus. When we think our offering is too small, let us remember my friend Brenda and the power of a small seed to move mountains. When we think it is too late, let us remember the story of the Cross and how, in his final hour, Jesus saved the life of a thief. It is never too hard, never too small, and never too late to love like we are dying. We are a withering blade of grass, a fading flower, a mist that dissolves into

193

the wind, but we are His finest creation, created for His joy, and rooted in His love. Thus we must now go, go and bear Him much fruit. As He has loved us, we must now love others. It is time to pick up our cross and follow Him. It is time to love like we are dying.

"Therefore, since we have been justified through faith, we have peace with God through our Lord Jesus Christ, through whom we have gained access by faith into this grace in which we now stand. And we boast in the hope of the glory of God. Not only so, but we also glory in our sufferings, because we know that suffering produces perseverance; perseverance, character; and character, hope. And hope does not put us to shame, because God's love has been poured out into our hearts through the Holy Spirit, who has been given to us. You see, at just the right time, when we were still powerless, Christ died for the ungodly. Very rarely will anyone die for a righteous person, though for a good person someone might possibly dare to die. But God demonstrates his own love for us in this: While we were still sinners, Christ died for us."

Paul the Murdered, but by Grace- Now the Apostle

A special thanks to my past and present iron: Timex, Kevin, JP, Josh, Adam, Steve, Jim, Hadden, Chip, Waldo, Scott, Jason, Blake, John, and countless others who have sharpened me.

Afterword

I thought it was important to add a note about why I used quotes from several films that have content that is not conducive to Christian living. I am not necessarily proud that I myself have been so impacted by secular entertainment, but regardless, it is part of my personal story. I thought honesty and the use of familiar references would be helpful for stimulating thinking as the conversation grew. Like music, film is a way of story telling and sometimes it is graphic. The Bible is also graphic at times, and I think this adds to the familiarity of the story that mirrors our own lives. I do openly admit that most films are not a great source for true wisdom, but some do contain central truths about life and God. I would never condone anyone looking to validate truth searching anywhere but in the Word of God. I would urge parents to use extreme caution while trying to create an environment conducive for spiritual growth for young people. I personally would not keep things in my house that could make the ones I love stumble. Whatever is noble, whatever is pure, whatever is true, think on these things.

Timm Hammer Jonson

A Donut Under Construction

Contact Information

Timm currently owns Java Café and Green Frog Coffee Co. Single, thus far, he focuses his life on leading coed small groups, teaching in his church, event speaking, writing, weather forecasting, attending morning men's groups, and working on developing a discipleship program in his hometown. To reach Timm for event speaking, including weekend retreats, or to attend a small group Bible study please call:

731-377-9684

timmhammerjonson@aol.com

 **TIMM HAMMER JONSON**

OR

GREEN FROG COFFEE CO

 **TIMMHAMMER**

 **timmhammerjonson**

www.greenfrogcoffeeco.com

CHAINSAW PREACHER

"A True Story"

BY TIMM HAMMER JONSON

AVAILABLE AT WWW.GREENFROGCOFFEECO.COM
or any Green Frog Coffee Co location

This book is for the overwhelmed cheerleader and the overlooked tuba player; the timid student and the tired teacher; the secret addict and the silent victim; the criticized sinner and the critical church; the lost child and the lonely adult; the new believer and the never ending skeptic; the bleeding wounded and the blessed Healer; and for the fragile fallen who can't get up.

It will be a lot of things to a lot of people: a story about a boy wounded early in life; a tale about a minister struggling with addiction; a song about a sinner who learns about grace; a mystery about a man who meets God by meeting others; but most important, it is my true story. It is the path through, and to, all those other horrible and beautiful things.

PREFACE

Many Christian books are over the head of common people like my self. Why? Maybe because they use too many big words and often don't write about "real" life experiences.

I tell this story in plain language. When God came in the flesh He walked among us sharing stories and parables. I've also chosen to wrap the truth about my life in a series of short personal stories. This book is a collection of those stories.

Some of my stories are silly, lighthearted tales, while others are serious spiritual discussions. Just as the Bible shares details about sexual sin, a few of my stories also contain mature sexual themes.

Telling the truth is hard. Telling the whole truth about your life is scary. A girl named Jenni asked me if I was excited about telling this story. I told her I was scared people wouldn't love me if they really knew me. But as I was writing this book I discovered a diamond of truth in the rough part of baring my secrets: unless people really know us, they can't love us.

One way we can show our love for others is by trusting them enough to reveal who we really are. These are the true stories of my life – shared with you. I hope you find this experiment helpful.

"Confess your sins to one another
and pray one for one another so you can be healed."
James 5:16a

This story would not be possible without all the people I have written about giving me permission to talk about what's wrong with them as I talk about what's wrong with me. On behalf of everyone who will be ministered to by the truth, I thank you for your courage and the gift you gave me in allowing me to share your story as I share mine. The true testimony of this book is that all of us agreed on staking our reputation on the truth. Our prayer is that God is going to use it.

*Some names have been changed to protect friends I could not find or who choose to remain anonymous.

Lost & Wounded

CANDY COATED

The Bible opens with a nude scene.

Although I was surrounded by some of the kindest people I've ever met in Sunday school, I feel like they failed to tell me the truth, but not intentionally, and not because they didn't love me. They probably felt like they were doing me a favor by editing the graphic nature of God's relationship with man.

Fortunately I found out later in life God prefers telling the truth and telling all of it. Telling a true story requires telling the good and the bad. Omit any one piece or page and it can ruin the ending. I love the stories God tells because He believes in full disclosure.

The Bible reveals sensitive secrets. Genesis tells us our first polygamist emerges just shortly after our firstborn son Cain kills his younger brother Abel. It tells us Noah, after being cooped up on that boat for almost a year, got buck naked drunk and fell asleep where his youngest son proceeded to make fun of him. When Noah woke up he did what a lot of dads do: he started cursing.[1]

I was told the story of Noah and the animals but they always left the drunk part out; just like they left out the part about Abraham having a wife so beautiful he was afraid someone would kill him just to sleep with her. So to keep his head attached to his shoulders, Abraham told everybody she was his sister and didn't seem to mind that other men might have sex with his wife.[2] They also left out the part about him sleeping with the maid and concubines too.

Other parts were also conveniently skipped. I never heard about how Lot's daughters, desperate for children, got their own father drunk so they could have sex with him. Not just one night, but two. Both got pregnant.[1]

1. Genesis 9:24-25   2. Genesis 12:10-20

The stories I heard left out the murders, the nude scenes, and the sexcapades. They were edited.

On the cutting room floor of appropriateness was that Judah mistakenly slept with his son's widow who he thought was a prostitute[2]; that holy Moses killed a man and hid the body[3]; that king David was a peeping Tom who valued sexual gratification over a man's life[4]; that Solomon probably slept with more women than Wilt Chamberlain really ever did[5]; and that rather than telling Hosea to avoid Vegas, God told him to marry a prostitute.[6] These details were, I guess, considered too mature for a younger audience.

I really begin to think about the true stories God is telling when I showed, ironically, an edited clip of The Passion to some of my middle school friends. A father was outraged that I had exposed his twelve-year old daughter to the violence of the crucifixion. At the time I agreed with him that I had crossed a line, used poor judgment, and learned my lesson, but luckily I thought about it more.

The Passion isn't violent enough. The real story says he wasn't recognizable as a human being.[7] It says the beating was so bad you had to stare at him just to figure out who or what he was. I grew up thinking the man had a good whipping and took a nap for a few days. I now know He endured a physical torture beyond my comprehension. Whereas the G-rated version led me to make crosses out of popsicle sticks, the R-rated version of the story saved my life.

The problem for me was I grew up in a Christian world of edited stories and pictures. I grew up staring at a good looking, muscular, Caucasian man with a beard trimmed and waxed. I found out the true story reveals the picture was a fake. He wasn't attractive, and this alone would have meant the world to me in adolescence when my body started looking like Mr. Potato Head with a few pieces in the wrong place.[8]

2   1.Genesis 19:30-38   2. Genesis 38   3. Exodus 2:11-14   4. 2Samuel 11
      5. 1Kings 11:3   6. Hosea 1:2   7. Isaiah 52:14   8. Isaiah 53:2

Even the people who surrounded me were edited. As a child I thought the people I went to church with all went home to perfect families, all paid their taxes, and all only had sex to produce children. Like the Dick Van Dyke show, I thought they slept in two separate beds. I believed the church, the community in which I should have felt most at ease, was a place for perfect people. As I evolved into my sinful nature, I simply believed there was something wrong with me even Jesus couldn't fix.

Although I'm sure my church family had real problems, I can't remember anyone ever really talking about the real details of their life. To talk, you had to walk down front at the end of the service while everybody stared as you privately discussed your needs and sins with your pastor. At times people said stuff out loud but no one ever got up front and said, "*I cheated on my wife, I'm an alcoholic, or I'm addicted to porn.*" It would have also meant the world to me to know that God uses people who make mistakes; that we come from a flawed stock of spiritual heroes; that if we mess up, get drunk, cuss, have sex, or even get pregnant, we can still be part of a powerful story that makes a difference.

I remember we took attendance, offering and Bible reading so seriously we posted them on boards in front of the church. But what we didn't take seriously at times was the truth, the truth about each other; probably because we were scared that our sinful habits were unique, isolated events; or probably because we feared disclosure, or a plea for help, would make people predisposed to think of us as the unsuccessful Christian. Our fear kept us from allowing ourselves to really be loved because we were always aware that those who said they loved us actually loved the person we invented, not the real person inside.

Our worst nightmare was that someone might find out who we really were. Stephen King made this nightmare into a film with his 1999 miniseries _The Storm of the Century_ where a once in a lifetime blizzard besieges Little

3

Tall Island off the coast of Maine cutting the small fishing community off from all contact with the mainland. A murder takes place and the perpetrator is jailed but then a series of mysterious suicides take place. The townspeople soon discover the man behind the bars is telepathically responsible and also possess a unique supernatural power: He knows all the sins everyone has ever committed.

He starts messing with people by openly discussing how they cheated on college exams, beat a homosexual up, and slept with an out of state prostitute while their mother was dying on her death bed. He tells the town constable, *"Your town is full of adulterers, pedophiles, thieves, gluttons, murderers, bullies, scoundrels, and covetous morons, and I know every last one of them."*

When I was a child in church we seemed to believe this villain, the secret bearer, might be each other. We acted as if telling the truth would be the equivalent of painting a big red bull's eye on our heart inviting people to take cheap shots. Our fear kept us silent. Our fear kept me lonely.

This is why I am telling this story, my story, unedited and raw; because I believe there is something special about the truth and rather than saving paint, we do it, and us, a great injustice when we try to clean it up. I also believe we redeem our story, our life, when we tell it the way it happened and not the candy coated version. We need to tame our sugar tooth and swallow our medicine. Our life is not some airbrushed, edited picture we market to public opinion; sometimes it's the ugly truth we share. If you don't mind, I'd like to share mine truthfully with you.

PEEING IN THE POOL

Some people say we drive our parents crazy.
Mine got there fast. I drove a Ferrari.

At the age of three I had my first experience in a public swimming pool as my mother was having her last. Up until this summer all my water excursions had been in unsanitized ponds, lakes, and creeks. I was held gently but firmly by the shoulders, looked directly into my little green eyes, and instructed if I wanted to go to the bathroom, unlike all the times before, I would need to get out of the water. I bobbed my head back and forth signaling I had understood. I am "told" a series of events then unfolded. Personally, I have no memory of any lewd behavior before the age of five.

As I understand, not long after arriving, my mother proceeded to go down the slide where, at the bottom, she started to kick and spit in a fit of drowning while in two feet of water because she didn't realize she could just stand up. Terrified of the shallow end, she vowed to never swim again and has kept that promise. But what was unfolding at the other end of the pool, trumped her near death experience.

A slow roar of chatter begin to build as everyone started pointing and moving out of the pool as my family turned to see little Timmy standing at the opposite end, trunks covering his bare ankles, playing fountain with his lily back into the pool. I was following my set of instructions. I was out of the pool standing clearly on dry ground (any good attorney would have taken my case). In my young innocent brain I must have thought city people had a cool way of shaking the dew off their lily. And better yet, with everyone staring at me and pointing, I was probably thinking they had never seen that much dew.

Perhaps this is what I loved most about my childhood, the temporary who cares attitude. Who cares if I suck my thumb after I pick my nose? Who cares if I eat jellybeans I find between the car seats in July? Who cares if my mother spits on a Kleenex and washes my face? Who cares if my shoes don't match? Who cares if I kiss my father? Who cares if I believe in Santa? Childhood's ability to dodge the poisonous darts of comparison preserved our innocence and gave us the presence of mind to keep eating cookies with our pants full of crap.

But I did care about some things. I cared about ice cream. Ice cream mattered to me, mattered so much I was willing to steal to get it.

In kindergarten I usually hated ice cream break because I rarely ever had the ten cents to buy it. I'd sit there and watch Rowland or Shanie enjoy their ten minutes of frozen kisses from God while my mouth just watered and my body went into diabetic shock. One day my luck changed when my teacher, Mrs. Chatham, mysteriously had an extra fudge bar left over. She raised it up asking who didn't get their ice cream. No one claimed it, so I did! I was giving my gift from God a good lovin' of French kisses when Keith came back from the bathroom looking for his ice cream. I heard Mrs. Chatham say something about raise our hand if we got Keith's fudge bar but I was too busy wolfing it down, hiding the evidence. Unfortunately for me she had retained a list of paying customers and my name wasn't on it. I took a note home that day, my summons to appear in the court of the principal's office.

Ice cream wasn't done with me yet. My mother kept a jar of miscellaneous pocket jargon in the laundry room including spare change recovered from the pants of three kids and a husband. There in that jar was a lifetime supply of frostbite for my lips. After consulting my stuffed dog, Henry, I formulated a plan. It would be a sunrise attack.

I went through my morning routine of begging for a dime from The Resistance and, once I had confirmed a "no can do," I

The Resistance- my mother

conveniently took some clothes to the laundry. She'd never miss a dime. How could she? It was like walking into a neighbor's yard and taking a blade of grass. Later that afternoon, as soon as I came through the door, she asked, *"How was the ice cream?"*

I underestimated The Resistance. There were no razors under the fingernail, no rats chewing on my ears and no sawdust in my eyes. It was much worse. I was grounded from a Halloween party.

There were other things worth risking my life for: Stickers! My mother used to buy bread by the truck load and freeze it. I think it was a quirk in her personality as a survivor of the great depression. When we needed a loaf we would grab it from the freezer and let it thaw out. Wonder Bread had these great Super Hero stickers at the end of the loaves that my two sisters and I would fight over just like the freebies in cereal boxes. So one day, when everybody else was busy outside, I went to the freezer and took all the frozen bread and dump it out of the plastic bags onto the floor to get the stickers (the early bird gets the worm). Then I tried to stuff all ten loaves back into the plastic bags but they didn't really fit for some reason. You would think there would be more room without the stickers. However sloppy it looked, it worked. I had my stickers and everybody else had floor trash on their toast. At the age of five I would have mowed your grass for a couple of stickers a week. It would have been between you and me, no I.R.S.

School was ok but I lived for summer, well maybe sugar. I loved to take fresh strawberries and a big bowl of sugar and climb up on the sofa where I was prepared to scream like somebody was sticking an ice pick in my belly button if anyone told me to share with somebody. I learned very early in life that sugar and my heart must both be guarded.

7

Sugar was best suspended in carbonated water in fructose form, especially in a cold glass bottle of Coke. On a hot summer day I would struggle to hold the giant bottle as the cold drops of condensation rolled down my chest as I nursed from God's reserve (the analogy is for sell Coca-Cola). Drinking a coke was easy. Getting a Coke was the hard part.

A long mile from our house down a country road was a small store we would walk to and scavenge for discarded glass bottles for refunds in ditches along the way. The store would give us ten cents a piece for them. Every time I picked one up I thought, *"Who would throw away ice cream?"*

We usually wound up with fifty cents or so a piece, enough for a Coke, a Chick-a-stick, candy cigarettes and a Thousand Dollar Bar. I'd eat all mine on the way home, whereas my sisters would taunt me with their disciplined rationing for the next five days. My sisters kept Halloween candy until Thanksgiving. Mine was gone November 1st **(the first hint in my life that I despised discipline).**

Summer also involved the art of canning, or, as I now understand it, working your cushion off for a pint of

Cushion- human buttocks; backside: gluteus maximus

relish. I snapped beans, shelled peas, shucked corn, pulled potatoes, pickled tomatoes, picked strawberries, peeled apples, boiled jars and melted wax all for the wage of a sticker.

There was one fringe benefit: a hot, fresh vat of strawberry jam, gallons of it, feet deep. When no one was looking I would stick my arm in it down to my hairless pit and run outside behind the house where I'd lick it off for the next fifteen minutes like a cat. Don't knock it until you try it!

Then there were the glorious sounds of summer. I remember the faint roar of Guy Lundy's crop dusting plane heading in my direction, calling me to the garden where I stood armed with dirt clods trying to take the ace pilot down. He would tease me with aerobatics and fly-bys as I would chunk pieces of earth at his airship with no regard for his family.

I recall the sound of my father's truck door slamming shut as he arrived home at noon, signaling it was time for a hot lunch (vegetables taste like heaven when your cushion is in them).

I'd like to forget the occasional one hundredth of a second ping of ripping metal as the stupid chain on my swing broke sending me bleeding and crying into the comforting arms of my mother.

My mother's voice called me away from tree house construction, called me down from the apple tree for a switching, and called me by my full name when I resorted to throwing bricks at friends who tried to cheat me out of my bat in softball.

I was serenaded by the hum of mowers feeding my allergies, the whining of home made ice cream makers (the voice of God), and the occasional startling high octave cursing of someone whose foot found a bee always followed by the stench of vinegar.

When the sun sank like a ship beyond the trees, I heard the sweet tenor of frogs waiting to pee on my hands; the sound of grasshoppers waiting to spit grass juice on my shirt; and the deafening silence of fireflies destined for hard time in the prison of my mayonnaise jar. I fell asleep to the purr of the attic fan pulling in the cool night air through my bedroom window along with gnats to fly into my eyes; the annoying *eeeek eeeek* of a cricket that was planted by Satan in the unknown crevice of my room; the *scritchy scratch* of a mouse nesting in my wall growing babies who would leave their cute little feces in my shoes; the sound of thunder reminding me I had left the B copy of the encyclopedia out in the yard where I had referenced the article on baseball to determine the right amount of distance to stand from home plate before I struck my sister in the face with the ball; and the sweet sound of rain whisking me away to dreams of helicopters delivering bales of candy to my house and dropping them precisely on a cricket and a mouse.

But summer would pass by all too quickly and again it was time for school. School was a hard place for me, for anyone who stutters. In a place where intelligence is often portrayed as the one who raises their hand to answer questions there is little opportunity for those who, although they know the answer, can't spit it out. It is highly frustrating for a child who stutters to be overlooked by teachers as well as laughed at by peers. The taunting of older kids only made the matter worse. Ironically I made perfect grades but hated reading because I had to read out loud which was something I simply couldn't do. In math I was put in a special group for gifted children while in reading I was put in a special group for those who were challenged. A long yard stick awaited my hand when I failed to deliver with perfection the sentences I could easily say out loud without the pressure of an audience. The summer after first grade I read fifteen books at the county library to catch up with my peers but more than anything to escape the yardstick. But just when the challenge of school became overwhelming, the Christmas catalogue would arrive in the mail.

By instinct, the day after Thanksgiving we'd drag out our fake tree, snap it together, throw on ten pounds of tinsel, plug in the lights, and instantly crave sugar.

Unique to the season were bags of orange slices, books of lifesavers, cartons of chocolate cherries, mugs of boiled custard, canes of peppermint, and sheets of fudge. Sugar and Jesus, a match made in heaven.

I must confess there was one thing I hated about Christmas: our gingerbread house. Constructed before I was ever born, perfectly preserved, it taunted me with its roof of gumdrops and yard of white frosting. Every time I walked by it I eyed it like a hawk honing in on a weak field mouse. Like the Big Bad Wolf chasing the three little pigs, I'd verbally assault the structure. Under my breath I cursed the day it was made as my mouth watered and legs began to shake. It stood like the Ark of the Covenant in my living room, like the tree of Good and Evil in the garden of Eden, touch but do not taste. I was like an alligator forced to peacefully coexist with a meaty chicken. I hated that house and one by one, year after year, I began to disassemble it one sweet, old, hard gum drop at a time. It served the chicken right!

The only thing better than Christmas vacation was an unexpected snow day. All snow that fell from 1974 to 1987 was via God trying to shut me up. I prayed for snow more than I prayed for my sins to be forgiven. I absolutely loved the stuff, maybe because it reminded me of ice cream and sugar. I'd wake up early, crawl over to the window, blink a few times, confirm the road was covered and then patiently sit by the radio waiting to hear, "*Madison County Schools will be closed today.*" I paused for two seconds out of reverence for the sacred gift and then scrambled around the house looking for gloves and boots, grabbed my Flexible Flier and headed for the steepest hill I could find that didn't feed me into a briar patch or a barb wire fence. I'll go ahead and tell you: My sled got the part of my cushion the relish left.

We had been out sledding, ripping into one another in heated races, when it ripped into me. I had just returned from making a simple repair to the pivot bolt in the center of the steering bar. I could not find a bolt so I used the next best thing- a huge, fat, five inch wood screw pointing up! (My lawyer told me to tell you I was in a hurry)

We were racing down a hill on Campbell Lane where, while I was gone, the sun had peeped out and exposed a bare spot on the pavement. Unaware of the danger, I sat down, planted my feet on the front, pulled back on the

11

rope and headed for the bottom. I reached top speed at precisely the moment my sled came to an immediate halt on the now dry patch of asphalt (the need for anti-lock brakes apparent). I got my first physics lesson when the inertia of my body continued to move forward while the screw dug a trench in my cushion.

I rolled about ten feet and came to a stop face down in the snow. I took my hand, patted my backside and pulled my blood soaked glove back around to my face where I visually confirmed the causality. My sister trotted over, looked at my cushion, then looked at me and said, *"You need surgery."*

With a six-inch gash in my left cheek and the fat hanging out, I limped back home. I laid on my stomach on our couch where my parents inspected the wound and heard my father say, *"Get me some duct tape."*

So there I was in childhood beginning to assemble some truths about life, learning it is easy to miss the point and hard to miss the pool, and we learn a great deal through our mistakes. When we are stung, spanked, or scarred the truth that our beautiful planet is cursed introduces itself to our feeble ability to grasp the horror. We deal with it by crying. We cry when we can't have a cookie, when we spill our milk, and when we skin our knee. Yet we weep when our dog dies, when our grandfather is lying in a wooden casket unable to speak, and when we begin to understand perfection is just a myth out of reach to those who stand in the shadows of giants.

Since the Enemy visited me at a tender age, maybe the unedited version of the truth should have too. If something was going to bite me, I needed to at least be forewarned. And nothing would have exposed the seriousness of the Enemy's assault better than the graphic truth about the bloody price of my redemption. It might have scared me to death to hear it, but at least I would have known to run.

12

TIMEX & JOAN OF ARC

They didn't give me everything I wanted,
but they gave me everything that mattered.

I still remember the day I discovered my father was flawed. We were sitting in an old, dusty pickup parked in the middle of our farm's gravel road talking to my Uncle while he was checking his mail. A few of our African American dairy hands, who lived in block houses, pulled up behind us in a car waiting to get through. My father and uncle ignored them and continued their conversation. A horn was honked and words were exchanged but we did not move. I was sitting in the seat, my legs not touching the floorboard, getting nervous, wondering why we didn't just pull over to the side. I looked at my father and realized he wasn't perfect. It was a truth not easy to swallow.

In reflection I think if I had known all along what his weakness was, or that he even had one, I would have handled it totally different. When I watched Superman on TV fall apart because of a green rock called kryptonite I felt sorry for him, in part because I anticipated it would happen. This weakness with my father, deacon of the church, surprised me. If felt more like I'd just found out I was adopted and didn't know who my father really was.

A couple of years later my mother showed me her fangs. It was the week before mother's day and I was tired of presenting pieces of paper, glued and glittered. I wanted to build something. I had heard her talk about wanting a rose trellis. So with my tree house experience and what little knowledge of trellises I had, I commenced construction. I had been working for a couple of hours, making progress, when she emerged on the scene. She took one

13

good glance at my project and said, *"I don't want that ugly thing in the yard."*

I was crushed beyond belief. With tears in my eyes, I flew into a rage and turned to see her walking away. I threw a two by four at her narrowly missing her head. She never looked back. I wept as another great dose of the truth was shoved down my throat. My mother wasn't perfect either.

I love my parents. I love them dearly and I will tell you why. At the tender age of adolescence we do not grasp the fact that, like most things in life, our family is simply a reflection of God not God himself. God uses our father, our mother, our brothers, and our sisters along with other people in our life to subliminally remind us of our sacred roots and our heavenly home. These reflections are not perfect, but they are powerful. My parents were Timex and Joan of Arc.

Timex- notoriously tough watch reasonably priced

Joan of Arc- Christian martyr that was burned at the stake

James Johnson; a.k.a Frog; the oldest son of a successful yet sometimes distant father; a child of the great depression; a child who grew up in a culture that referred to African Americans as niggers; a teenager who picked cotton by hand; a teenager who patrolled strawberry patches carrying a gun; a man who served his country in the United States Army; a man who was an eye witness to desegregation; a man who built his own house; a man who was a workaholic; a man who was considered a good catch; a man of few words but delightfully funny at times; a man who throws nothing away; a farmer and a firefighter; and a man I respect.

First and foremost, my father was the one who determined what constituted professional medical care in my family. The standard as I now understand it is a limb must be fully detached. I was always mesmerized at his Timex toughness, his ability to *"take a lickin' and keep on tickin'."*

I have heard before I was born he pushed a metal pipe through his hand and drove himself to a clinic where the receptionist fainted when shown the injury. He's tough like a two-dollar steak.

Once while hanging paneling I accidentally nailed him in the forehead with a hammer instantly turning him into a unicorn stunt double. He refused to go to the doctor. He's tough like a cafeteria corndog.

Chainsaws always had a way of getting him into trouble. One crisp October day we were cutting firewood and, at the disapproval of my mother, I was running a smaller red version of my dad's green McCullough or "the beast" as I called it. The tree was down and I was busy sawing off leaves or something with my miniature version when I suddenly found myself lying on the ground and out of breath.

My father had cut a main branch about three feet in diameter unaware I was underneath it with my tiny red saw giving some leaves heck. He saw me out of the corner of his eye as I went down. He rushed over, scooped me up in his arms, and put me on the tailgate of the truck. I remember looking into his eyes and seeing fear for the first time, or as I now understand, compassion. He watched me struggling to breathe and began asking if I was ok, where it hurt, etc. Following in his footsteps, as air slowly seeped back into my lungs, I hoarsely whispered, *"IIII'mmm fffiinneee."* He responded, *"We'll don't tell your mother."*

We agreed that a near death experience was something that can upset a woman so we reached an understanding, loaded up, and headed home. I was stiff and tried my best to walk normally to the shower shucking clothes as I went. Just as I was soaped up enjoying the soothing warmth of the water I

heard my mother say, *"WHERE IS ALL THIS BLOOD COMING FROM!"*
The limb had split my back open. I stood frozen, naked, soap in hand, when
I said, *"I don't know."* I felt sorry for my father who strategically dismissed it
as a superficial wound.

Around this time a wager emerged in our home. If my mother lost twenty
pounds, the Chinese chestnut tree she so despised would be cut down. I
referred to it as the Devil Tree. It had beautiful waxy leaves, perfectly shaped
limbs, and was the best shade tree in the yard. The problem was it produced
a chestnut covered in spines. Needles that is! Darn sharp too! You'd be
enjoying a game of tag or hide and seek, clutching a Push Up, running
through the soft cool grass with bare feet thinking, *"I love you Lord, thank
you for this day, my friends, my life and ...WHAT THE #$%!?"*

There in the bleeding sole of your foot was one of those darn chestnut
skins buried fast and hard. So it was easy to see why I was happy when my
mother won the wager.

My father proceeded to cut Satan back to just the central main trunk but it
was precariously close to the house. He recruited me and my sister to pull on
a rope attached to the top of the tree which would hopefully swing the main
trunk away from the roof and back toward the concrete driveway. So there
we were pulling on this rope, my skinny mother on the sidelines, and my dad
forty feet up in the air holding onto a stub of a branch with one hand and
using a big chainsaw with the other.

The next five seconds were slow motion. My dad lost his grip, grunted,
and cascaded down the tree for a few feet then began a free fall descent that
ended with him landing on his back on the concrete still holding the
chainsaw. I had just witnessed the death of my father.

16

Chris started crying, I started weeping and my mother said, *"Oh Jamie!"* Then the miracle happened. He grunted, checked the choke on the chainsaw and climbed back up the tree to finish the job. It was the pinnacle of his Timex personality.

Later that night I remember seeing him in front of the bathroom mirror checking his cracked ribs and his back now black and four shades of blue. I thought, *"Hurts, doesn't it?"*

My dad taught me a no holds barred approach to life. He was always willing to assume risk for reward, to build it before buying it, and show me rather than say it.

Once while working, we parked the truck, got out, and turned around to see it rolling down a hill toward a tree about forty yards away. Surprised, I looked over at my father who was already giving chase. I stood there, wanting popcorn, as I watched the greatest short action film of my life.

He ran like the wind that day. Pulled up along side the truck in stride, grabbed the door handle, and jumped inside just in time to make the impact. His whole body lurched forward and gathered itself on the dashboard. The door opened and he stumbled out, inspected the damage, hopped back in and parked it horizontally across the slope.

I can remember few times in my life when my dad told me he loved me but I'll never forget the times he showed me. Especially December 19, 1975

It was the end of the school semester and I was happily on my way home on the bus with my Christmas party candy stashed securely in a cigar box. I hated the bus more than the gingerbread house.

I was a minority, a white child among several African Americans, and I received what my ancestors had devastatingly dished out. I was an easy target with ears so big I looked like a car going down the road with both doors open. I would sit and stare straight ahead waiting for the stinging thumps to my ears to begin. In a way I understood their discontent and need to vent their frustration. We, the white community, tried our best to make them feel inferior. I just hated that it was my ears that gave them a refund.

I want to pause here and tell you my guardian angel was black not white. His name was Sylvester Tippler. He was one of the many of our poor farm hand's children. Like most of them, he was a kind spirit but different in the fact that he was much older, huge, and athletic. He went on to play college football and became an asset to a community. If I was lucky enough I got to sit in close proximity to him on the bus where, because he defended me, the abuse didn't take place. But this day I found myself sitting in the back, staring forward, waiting.

I was surprised when the knife settled across my throat but shocked at the demand, *"GIVE ME YOUR CANDY DUMBO!"* I couldn't believe the bully! He could have told me to strip or to kill the bus driver, but my candy? He had nerve!

I quickly remembered hearing that some things in life are worth fighting for and thought, *"This is it!"* With a knife under my Adam's apple, I slipped my hand into my cigar box as if I was going to be an easy take down but instead firmly gripped a pair of Snoopy scissors. With a quick turn and a twist I had stabbed a man, an eleventh grader. With blood trickling from the hole and the news of the surprise attack spreading from seat to seat the bus came to a screeching halt. I escaped punishment, candy intact.

I got off the bus, walked inside, and burst into tears as my sisters informed my mother why there was a red mark on my neck. A few minutes

18

later my father walked in and asked what all the commotion was about. He looked at my neck, turned red, went into the bedroom, and returned to the kitchen loading two pistols. He strapped one to his ankle and one to his waist and said, *"I'll take care of this once and for all."* We all looked at each other and started crying. Our father was going to prison.

What he said or what he did remains a mystery. All I know is that from that day forward there was a new respect for me on the bus. Maybe they considered me wild and dangerous, maybe my father pistol-whipped a few folks, or maybe he hid the body like Moses. But

> **Dumbo-** a Disney cartoon elephant that used his ear like wings to fly
>
> **Pistol-Whip-** beating someone using a gun as a blunt object

one thing was for sure: from that day forward I realized, like God, my father valued my life more than his own.

Timex had a soft side too. My mother knew where it was. I vividly remember the two fights they had, the two where we as children huddled together believing divorce was imminent.

The worst of these involved money during a very stressful time when my father was trying to make ends meet. My mother, looking through some insurance papers, said, *"You're worth more dead than you are alive."* I honestly think it hurt him more than anything she ever said. It questioned his validity as a provider, his soul as a man. I quit listening when the shouting started and started trying to concentrate on which one of my parents I would want to live with. Somehow they worked it out like some married couples do who figure out how to love each other deeply enough to bridge the faults. The other fight put us all in a tent on weekends.

My father was playing softball and was gone a few nights a week. My mother, alone at home with three kids, confronted him about his role as a father. A fight erupted and Terry, Chris, and I headed for the *"who am I going to live with"* huddle waiting for the bell to signal the end of round one. The end came quickly, with a knock out punch I guess.

The conclusion was we would start camping and my father would say good-bye to softball. It was the boldest and wisest rope-a-dope my father ever pulled. We had fun camping and he never had to

> **S & H Green Stamps-**
> redeemable stamps
> received when buying
> groceries. Sort of like
> frequent flier miles.

compete again in his life. He has never even watched a single sporting event on television since. The two dollar steak quit cold turkey.

Ironically, it is my mother who now at the age of seventy-two can tell you the starting lineup of the Memphis Tigers and shakes the

> **Rope-A-Dope-** when
> someone in boxing
> pretends to be hurt

radio trying to pick up Cardinal baseball stations. My father prefers watching old westerns where they legally shoot people for cheating at cards and for taking candy from a baby. Maybe he should star in one?

Beverly Silkwood; a coal miner's daughter; a child of the great depression; a girl who walked to school; a girl who attended multiple funerals on Christmas day in 1951 when the Orient#2 coal mine exploded killing 152 men in her hometown of West Frankfort, Illinois; a woman whose secret ambition was to become a missionary; a woman who worked her way through college; a woman who learned to adjust to having a brother and sister who lived in a world of Schizophrenia; a woman who became a teacher but quit to become a mother; and a woman worn by her sacrifice but beautiful to those who received it.

My mother was the one who always found a way to stretch a dollar. Once a year she'd pull out the S&H Green Stamps and make us lick and stick booklets until our speech slurred from the paste. With a truckload of full books, we would go pick up our plastic saltshaker and dream about getting the peppershaker next year. She believed in saving.

She saved rubber bands from newspapers and paper bags from the grocery store. Plastic silverware was washed and reused. Pickle and peanut butter jars were rinsed and saved. If we made the mistake of leaving crumbs on our plate we were quickly reminded of the burnt black loaf of bread her mother had to eat as a child when they had no food. She believed tea was a great way to rinse a ketchup bottle to get that last bit of taste on your meatloaf. Waiting for us in the refrigerator after school was any cereal we might have left in our bowl before catching the bus. Cheerios were now the size of doughnuts and soft like liver. Bathwater was recycled. We prayed to go first. Thermostats were turned up in the summertime and down in the wintertime. We burned up on the fourth of July and froze at Christmas. Switches were off. Money was saved.

She walked into motherhood like Patton into Sicily. Recipes came out of her like fur out of a mange cat. She cooked with authority. I could rely on the fact that

Patton- five star general in World War II known for being brash, ornery & successful.

when I sat down at the table I'd be satisfied. Around ten in the morning she'd start boiling water and two hours later we would have five vegetables, a meat, and a dessert. The things we ate all had our cushion in them (well a few animals made a contribution too).

When we killed twenty chickens and sixteen rabbits in one day she never blinked. She just boiled more water. She never seemed to mind when her back porch was covered in pig parts while we were making sausage. She adjusted well to gathering her own eggs and growing her own steaks. She learned, or seemed to already know how, to cook anything we could pick, catch or shoot.

21

After her title fight, we began to go camping several times a year and she packed a grocery store in an ice chest. There was an endless supply of canned drinks, sandwiches and snacks. Like one of those funny cars the clowns get out of, I never found the end of the food. Supplies were plentiful too. She couldn't pull a rabbit out of a hat but I'll be danged if she couldn't always hand you a roll of toilet paper and a can of bug spray.

She was a walking hardware/beauty/grocery store. We could have won a scavenger hunt with just her purse. Inside were her traditional half sticks of gum (no whole sticks- we might accidentally taste the flavor), fingernail clippers, powder, loose change, butterscotch candy, keys to things we no longer owned, various green stamps, pencils, band-aids, a set of silverware, ketchup packets, and those funny round soft things with strings on them (tampons-I feel stupid having played with them in church).

I think laundry screwed with my mother's mind. You can imagine what it is like dealing with disappearing socks for five people. I first noticed it when she began to repeatedly say, *"I'll never get that out."* I'd fall down and grass stain my pants and she'd say, *"I'll never get that out."* I understood grass stain could be tough but later realized even when I splashed water on myself she would instinctively say, *"I'll never get that out."* Half her life was spent scrubbing my clothes and the other half telling me how she couldn't get it out.

Sometimes she still believes the Civil War isn't over, or at least that is the only way I can explain why she will lock the door behind me when I walk out to go get the paper. She keeps the blinds closed and the curtains drawn creating this cave like ambience. If a rebel soldier does wander into her living room I'm not worried because he won't stay long in a house that's eighty degrees in June. On his way out he can grab an arm load of Wal-Mart plastic bags and a handful of rubber bands.

I've caught her watching the same episode of Wheel of Fortune back to back on two different channels. I guess it makes the puzzles easier the second time. She deserves to watch TV at this late stage in life. Because of her, my life was a little bit like Mayberry even though she's the one my cousins call Aunt Bee.

I still remember the night she called me and told me how she became the first female stripper in the Baptist church. Her story topped the Joan of Arc stunt she pulled when she wore a fuzzy angora sweater to a wedding reception and got a little too close to some candles. She engulfed herself in a three second ball of flames. (She has always liked the spotlight)

Over the phone she described how, after speaking up front about foreign missions, the elastic in the waistband of her pants snapped in two. One minute she's talking about feeding hungry orphans and the next minute she is standing in church in her underwear. The problem was, being a bit heavy, having had open heart surgery, shoulder surgery, a knee replacement, and hip work, there was no instant recovery. She had to waddle over to a pew and take a seat to get her pants back around her.

She has always been fearless. Chin up she adjusted to what life handed her. Sure she has her quirks like her obsession with hunting spiders at night with a flashlight while everyone else is sound asleep. I can also overlook her keeping ginger snaps in the cookie jar while Oreos were stashed in her bedroom dresser, because with her charred sweater and pants down, tied to the stake of domestic engineering, she won a boy's heart.

While it may be true I never had everything I wanted because we were a one income family and while it may be true that I was usually a year behind in fashion and am missing a piece of my cushion, it is also true that all those things I thought I needed to make me happy are now stacked in ten cent piles at yard sales on Saturday mornings.

What survives the storm of time is not what brand of shoes were on my feet but rather that when I ran off the bus I ran into my mother's arms. What she has probably never understood is she was a missionary after all, and I'm the savage she civilized.

My father still has divine appointments with danger. He cut his fingertip off a few years back in the wood shop. He never went to the doctor. With it black and crusty, he said he was letting it heal from the inside out. He never went when he stuck his other hand in the wood chipper either.

My mom, who has an affection for confection, still hides candy bars in the freezer. She likes Diet Rite Cola and her body continues to betray her. She sleeps in a chair every night because of the pain in her back.

But in spite of all they never were, a few things maybe they should have never been, they found a way to give me everything that really ever mattered. I love them because I didn't starve. They always found a way to feed both my stomach and my heart.

SEX IN A CALF BARN
Risky Business

My first sexual experience was in a calf barn. It was the same barn where I smoked my first cigar and the same barn where I promptly threw up. It was a barn with bales of hay, a barn with weaning calves, and a barn with a magazine.

By this time in my life I had begun to figure out the Sears catalog could be used for something more than browsing for Christmas toys and school clothes. It had a lot to teach me about pretty girls in dressed in nighttime attire.

TV taught me a lot too. Television was full of flesh in the seventies. There were *Charlie's Angels, The Dukes of Hazard, Wonder Woman,* and the occasional Sunday night *James Bond* movie. *Hee Haw* taught me if you have cleavage you don't need to sing to be a part of country music. In the morning, five days a week, *The Price is Right* taught me the real value of nautical equipment in the final showcase. Even the commercials showcased sex.

The magazine I found in the barn took me from first grade to a PhD. It said "Playboy" and on the front cover was a *Hee Haw* girl

The Enemy- the devil and his army

but without her shirt on. I assume a farm hand accidentally left it in the barn thumbing through the pages while feeding the calves in the morning. I stared at it like Yogi Bear eyeing a picnic basket. I reached over, carefully picked it up, and shook hands with my Enemy.

Some would say I lost my innocence that day, got an education on the birds and the bees, or introduced Dick to Jane but I know now I met the

25

Enemy. The Enemy wasn't a naked girl, the absent minded farm hand, or even Hugh Hefner in a smoking jacket. Hugh just wanted to get rich but the Enemy.... the Enemy wanted to take my life.

Looking back it is easy to see how much my life changed that day. I remember riding my bike a few days later to the local landfill and rummaging through people's trash desperately looking for more pictures. There was this odd thirst that had to be quenched even if it meant digging through trash. I just needed more Turkish delight.

In C.S. Lewis' *Chronicles of Narnia* Edmund is befriended by the White Witch who is posing as the Queen and given a candy called Turkish delight. It is an enchanted version. Once eaten, a person craves it so much they cannot stop eating it. If allowed, a person would kill themselves shoving it down their throat. In Edmund's quest for more he betrays his brother and sister, jeopardizes Narnia, and finds himself imprisoned. He is willing to risk everything for a piece of candy. I was willing to risk everything for a magazine.

Ironically my days of scavenging for it only lasted a few months. My neighborhood friends Jeff and Larry were "lucky" enough to have a father and a brother who kept large quantities of magazines in their own homes. When I spent the night with Jeff we would wait for his dad to have a few beers and fall asleep so we could "borrow" a few books from his library. Yet what I really wanted was my own Dewey decimal system. I wanted to study the books, file them away in my memory, and have instant access to their pages. Larry gave me that chance.

We arranged a weekend camping trip to my grandfather's lake and Larry brought along a little of his brother's "reading material." We made the two mile journey with a lawnmower pulling a trailer. We needed a trailer because we were taking everything a young man needs for a great weekend-

26

assorted fishing gear, a grocery store and lots of flesh, uncooked and air brushed. We fished a little, ate a lot, and did a bit of "reading."

After we got back home and started unpacking, Larry discovered his library was not intact. We looked at each other, eyes as big as doughnuts, knowing immediately we were at Defcon One.

Defcon One- *our military's fully* armed status for a nuclear threat

Somewhere between the lake and my house was Miss September 1980 in full view, the wind probably having blown her open to the centerfold. We feared my elderly grandfather would bush hog her and scatter a thousand pieces of flesh into the virgin country air. It was imminent we quickly recover her before someone else did.

Larry took off on search and rescue while I played decoy and unpacked. When I was finished I took a shower where I had a better look at Miss September. That's right! My integrity went out the window. I had stolen it. While Larry was frantically running reconnaissance till nightfall, I was showered and in the front of the TV watching *Hee Haw*.

With this new acquisition I doubled my personal library. After I "borrowed" a few more from my friends I was almost in need of a card catalogue until my mother found my stash.

Like a darn revenuer smashing booze, she confiscated and destroyed my bounty of magazines and in place of them left me a letter. I found it one day after school and engaged her in a short, no eye contact, thirty second conversation as she demanded to know the location of my still. I gave up Jeff and Larry like a well gives up water. I moved on embarrassed but undeterred. Like an ant colony disturbed, I set out to rebuild my collection bigger and stronger. Already at the age of twelve I had lost control to the Enemy, **my distaste for discipline growing and getting dangerous.**

27

The Enemy really stepped it up a notch when a guy named Don moved into the neighborhood. He had a fancy thing called a satellite and with the help of a VCR he amassed a complete video library of porn. Once a week, unbeknownst to my parents, I would walk two hundred feet across the street to borrow three or four movies. Don, a thirty something year old man, thought it was cool to let a fourteen year old boy view his entire collection of X-rated tapes. But pretty soon I didn't need Don, Jeff, or Larry.

At the age of sixteen I was walking into adult sections of video stores and renting the latest releases all by myself. Tapes were so frequent in my VCR my secret was quickly impacting the people around me. Friends would borrow my VCR and I would forget to take the tapes out. My sisters would see the tapes. I would run into people I knew while shopping in adult sections of video stores. It was risky business.

To understand how fatal the wound was you have to know how well it was timed. I found the magazine the same summer I felt God was trying to tell me something about my life, thus revealing the Enemy's attack on my life was strategically planned. His attack on you was too. For me it was a four front assault; a magazine to seed me; friends to lead me; a new neighbor to feed me, and a life of shame to bleed me of self worth, self respect, and self control.

At the time I was very much immersed in Christian community. I lived with Christian parents, went to church three times a week and was very involved in church activities. In many ways I used my church participation as a means to compensate for my secret addiction to porn.

> *Judas-* the disciple whose betrayal led to Jesus' crucifixion

On the outside I looked like Jesus but on the inside I felt like Judas.

I was simply surrounded by what I thought was perfection. And I felt like the exception. I thought I was the first church boy to ever be addicted to looking at naked women.

On Sunday mornings when someone did occasionally decide to confide in the pastor during the invitation I thought they were confessing failures to read the Bible, turning in empty offering envelopes, or forsaking their diet plan. I didn't think anyone was a thief, a liar, and an addict like me.

There were several nights I'd lie in my bed and try to reconcile my life with what I felt like God was trying to tell me when I was ten years old. I'd recall my candy coated stories of all those faithful perfect people and cry myself to sleep. I felt like I just wasn't good enough.

What I had felt in my heart when I was ten was that God wanted to say something through me. I often wondered if my gift was writing, but it really didn't matter because I knew I was sinner. So with lighting bugs in a jar, a magazine in my drawer, a real monster under my bed, and tears on my pillow, I waved good-bye to the shallow end of life and jumped head first into the deep end without a clue how to swim.

THE BEAST OF BEAUTY

Very early in life girls discover our society gives privilege to the pretty. The pretty girl gets noticed, the pretty girl gets moved to the front and the pretty girl gets more love. If they're not pretty, or not the prettiest, a girl can feel second hand. They often try to medicate their insecurity with the pursuit of popularity, a safe assembly of friends, and a boyfriend who tells them what they want to hear.

Life starts out innocently enough with wearing a pretty dress or clips in their hair. The special attention and comments from adults about how cute they look introduces them to the idea that love could be related to looking their best. The better they look the more attention they get. It isn't that looking good is bad, it's the fact they think they have to look perfect for someone to love them that kills them. The pressure of physical perfection wounds many females.

Puberty brings with it an often fatal blow. Some girls' figures develop earlier and they get more attention from the boys. Girls look around and realize there is a variety of shapes and sizes but they are old enough to understand our sexually charged society demands one size fits all. They look at a billboard and there she is- five foot eight, a hundred and fifteen pounds, blue eyes, blonde hair, chiseled abs, full chest, toned arms, and perfect teeth. They turn on the television or pick up a teen magazine and there she is again. They try to look like her even if it means starving their self to death. They spend hours in the gym and in a tanning bed in pursuit of perfection but regardless of how close they get, they never feel like they fit.

Sadly, life has a way of always putting girls in a line and making them deal with the fear of getting picked- dating, beauty pageants, and school dances. They become obsessed with trying to look their best. They add a

30

pound and they feel like the world is staring. They get a zit and want to stay home from school. They feel like everyone is looking and nobody likes what they see. They feel like their appearance is up for a vote every time they walk out the door.

They look for an island, a safe place, a sense of security. They find it in a boyfriend but sometimes they pay the price. They use their body as bait and feel like a dirty Cinderella when he bites. Yet it's addictive because they get a tainted version of the attention their heart is craving. The price is high but they're willing to pay it. They swallow the lie that being deeply loved depends on the way they look and how far they will go.

The wound of not being chosen and the curse of being chosen too much, do the same thing to girls that pornography did to me: it makes them start doubting they're good. They doubt God loves them.

I understand why they feel like there is no alternative to giving in to sex with their boyfriend. I was addicted to looking at pictures. They're addicted to trying to look like one. Both of us need help.

I've talked to several girls who feel pressure to look perfect. I've also noted an alarming increase in the provocative dress of younger and younger girls. When a girl who is thirteen feels like she has to look twenty-one it can be dangerous. Girls often think sexually stimulating a guy validates females in our culture. Girls often feel the best way to do this is to make them selves available for sex.

It's a dangerous game to play when we consider the price is much more than the loss of virginity or the risk of an STD. The price of attaching self worth to sexual prowess can psychologically confuse a woman, crippling her for life. A teenage girl with low self-esteem looking for love can get pregnant. A female in her thirties with low self-esteem can believe a part of

31

love is letting a man beat her up. A woman in her sixties with low self esteem can stop believing love exists and start wounding others or even her self.

Every female needs to know an authentic loving relationship holds together because of commitment not physical attraction. Ever wondered why we love God when we have no idea what he looks like? We love him because He loved us first. True love doesn't have eyes, it's all heart. Every female needs to know a relationship with God holds together because of his sincere love for us not our appearance or performance.

"The LORD does not look at the things man looks at. Man looks at the outward appearance, but the LORD looks at the heart."

1 Samuel 16:7

"Your beauty should not come from outward adornment, such as braided hair and the wearing of gold jewelry and fine clothes. Instead, it should be that of your inner self, the unfading beauty of a gentle and quiet spirit, which is of great worth in God's sight."

1 Peter 3:3-5

Peter was not saying it is wrong to wear jewelry or makeup and to dress up with modesty, but rather he was making the point that women shouldn't be so focused on outward appearance that they neglect their inner spiritual growth. We can look airbrushed on the outside but feel like trash on the inside. We can look like Jesus but feel like Judas. We have a lot in common.

MARLBORO, ELVIS, CROCKETT & LUKE

"A friend is one soul living in two bodies."

... Aristotle

While on his deathbed John Donne wrote *"no man is an island entire of its self."* Life is bearable with a few good friends. They may dare us to stick our tongue to a frozen pole, pee on an electric fence, or throw a stone at a wasp nest; they may laugh at us when we *"talt lite diss"*, when we are peeing on our shoes, or when we emerge from our house with eyes swollen shut smelling like vinegar; but friends... friends are the dessert on the buffet of life.

My first true, good friend was a cigarette. I loved him, really loved him. I think about him often and I'll tell you why. On a dairy farm you can count on one thing: hard work. At a very early age I started helping haul hay in the summer. I ran behind a cotton trailer grabbing and throwing rectangle bales up to someone who would stack them. I then rode to the barn where I pitched the bales off the trailer up into the loft to be stacked again. Bales weighed anywhere from twenty-five to fifty pounds. On a good day we could move about a thousand bales. It was a hot and sweaty job.

To get from the field to the barn I normally crammed into the cab of a pickup truck with three or four other farm hands. Whether they couldn't afford it or just didn't use it, they didn't wear deodorant. It smelled like four men with salty skunks under their arms. It made me want to puke, but just before I did I'd hear the click of a lighter.

Nothing smells better than burning tobacco when you're in the cab of a truck with four sweaty men. It smelled better than bread baking,

Molly Drury- a cute girl in my high school that always smelled as good as she looked

better than Molly Drury in high school. It was heaven's scent, God's cologne. I love you Marlboro Man.

To this day I can be sitting at a red-light with my window down, smell a cigarette and all the old memories come back. I miss him and wish him well.

Larry was probably my closest ally. To this day I think he is the most sincere, trustworthy person I know. He has a big heart and a beautiful family. He's the kind of man I sometimes wish I could be.

He is probably best remembered for his Elvis impersonations. His mom even made him little copies of Elvis' costumes. He had a special trunk where he kept the little treasures.

I'd be out in my back yard getting a wheelbarrow load of firewood when I'd see a flash of light out of the corner of my eye and hear Larry singing, *"You ain't nothing but a hound dog."* Fifty yards away, at the age of eight, covered in sequins and glitter, standing on top of his own pile of firewood, big fat collar flapping in the wind, holding a hatchet for a make believe microphone, was Larry singing at the top of his lungs as if girls were crying at his feet. Believe it or not, it was actually an impressive performance.

His room was covered in Elvis posters. He even had a memorial candle constantly burning for a few weeks after the King's death in 1977. Larry had a deep respect for the King and I had a deep respect for Larry.

Larry and his family were generous. While at my house carbonated drinks were rare, you were handed one as soon as you stepped into his yard. He always had snacks and always offered before you asked. His family was easy to like and even easier to love.

He was with me on all my secret missions. He'd dress up like a state trooper while I played dead on the roadside to see how many cars we could get to stop and stare. Sometimes the blood was real like when we dug foxholes together. I almost killed him when I pegged him in the forehead with a shovel. There was more blood than the night Tate Lancaster scraped his nipple off because he forgot to duck my clothesline while playing a game of hide n' seek. He helped me look for Tate's shoe flung off by the impact. The next morning he was on top of his woodpile, in his purple and white suit, hatchet in hand, singing, *"Won't you be my teddy bear,"* when I looked up from my own pile of wood and saw Tate's shoe on top of my roof.

Larry disappeared one day, grounded for life. He'd been stealing people's mail. He had a pile of it stashed out in a cornfield. I remember feeling sorry for him and his life sentence but I wasn't as good a friend as Larry. I joined the other kids in the neighborhood and talked about how it served the convict right. I didn't have the nerve to do what I should have done. I should have confessed my own sins and moved Larry into a larger minority or, as I know now, a majority. I was not loyal to Elvis.

He made a come back a few months later and went on to become the first kid in our neighborhood to own a go-cart and later a motorcycle. Some people thought he was dangerous. I thought he was one of the few real friends I had.

Over the years we dug more holes, got into more trouble and lost more shoes but during that time he stopped being my friend and started being my brother.

35

Jeff was the guy who knew how to handle the ladies. He showed up at the bus stop donning a white linen blazer and a bright blue T-shirt. His hair would be slicked back and his skin a glowing bronze. The girls loved the *Miami Vice* country boy.

He always had big dreams. Our first joint fantasy other than marrying one of those girls in those magazines was to own our own diesel truck and drive around the country hauling chickens. A little later we decided the cash flow would be poor so we decided to start looking for rare coins with a metal detector. Eventually we settled on pursuing our own individual careers until he brought home this little bag of green stuff.

I'd never seen marijuana until Jeff showed it to me. I had heard it got girls pregnant and sent people to jail for rolling it up. I was around him a few times when he was toking but never tried it myself, mostly because of what I saw it do to him. He started thinking too hard about our money situation and tried to get me to partner with him to secretly grow fifty acres of Mary Jane on my grandfather's farm. He said he wanted to retire after that. I told him I'd seen what "prison" did to Larry.

Jeff was fun to be around and had a cool family. I'd spend the night at his house, play cards and drink Coke hours after my normal bedtime. His family was poorer but richer in many ways. They seemed to be more relaxed smoking their cigarettes and Wayne drinking his beer. There seemed to be less to worry about inside their concrete blockhouse. There was always time to play games and his parents would often join us. I still remember when we broke their window how it was a no fuss affair, whereas it would have been the end of the world at other houses. The Wilsons were the kind of people I'd want with me on a boat if I ever got stranded on a deserted island.

It's been a long time since I've heard from Jeff. I hope he stayed out of jail because I didn't.

R usty was the kid with the cool car and freckles. He had a high-pitched southern drawl and a big smile. He too, did well with the ladies.

Rusty had a red mustang that he borrowed from NASA. I'd hop in, he'd punch the petal, and we'd quickly hit warp speed. It was fun going fast, risking your life and watching puffs of burning oil smoke come through the air vent. Although we could get to Beech Lake (thirty miles away) in ten minutes, we couldn't always get back. His car pulled a funny trick called not starting. It left us stranded many times seemingly unaware that women waited for us in other parts of the world.

At some point his red rocket laid down and my convertible was also in the shop. Embarrassed to cruise our parent's vehicles, we decided to lower our female age bar a little and went skating.

After rolling around for a couple of hours competing with *New Kids On The Block* songs for girls' attention we called it a night and headed for the house. We were driving down a four-lane by-pass when Rusty pulled up in his four-cylinder four door and goosed it a little. I looked over at him from my four door eight-cylinder and saw him grinning. Knowing what he had in mind, I punched it and waved at him in my rearview mirror. We were weaving in and out of traffic like the Duke boys in Hazard County when Roscoe showed up, six Roscoes.

Roscoes- law enforcement

With blue lights flashing and guns drawn, they ran over, yanked us out of our grocery getters and pinned us across the hood of a patrol car. There

Love Poems- poems that I had written and kept in my car in the case of an emergency

we were, cheeks pressed against hot metal, staring in wonder at each other as they hand cuffed us and put us in the back seat of a patrol car. For the next fifteen minutes they tore our cars apart looking for drugs and alcohol but only found a few of my love poems. They found those intoxicating because they laughed.

I was still thinking it would soon be over and we would just get a ticket. I was thinking Daisy would show up in her jeep wearing those short shorts when the tow truck showed up. It wasn't Cooter. I don't know what happened after this because the patrol car we were sitting in started heading downtown to the police station.

There they took our fingerprints, wallets, belts and shoes then escorted us to a jail cell with a toilet and two metal beds. We were booked on state charges of drag racing.

We were sitting together in the cell contemplating our fate, awaiting our one phone call, praying we would get out before the torture started. I got my call first and phoned my brother-in-law, a sheriff's deputy. I was thinking he could pull some strings. The only string he pulled was the loose one on his shirt as he informed me his hands were tied. He also told me my father had decided I could stay there until my court date to teach me a lesson. Rusty's phone call to his parents got the same result. There was a unified front.

We sat there like Paul and Silas waiting for a miracle but we weren't singing. We were rehearsing our defense for when we went before the judge to make sure our stories matched. Seven hours later in the morning, thanks to a bail bondsman, I left Rusty to fend for himself. He escaped (was bailed out) about six hours later.

Our jail visit held our dating game up a bit but it didn't stop us from raising cane (skating) in twelve counties and three states. I saw him the other day and we started laughing about our criminal record. In prison you make friends and enemies. I made a friend for life.

38

My friends did often get me into trouble but they also got me into the habit of being real with people. Growing up with these "sinners" I learned the Bible says Jesus had friends like these. It was easy to understand why. They were real. Maybe real funny, maybe real poor, or maybe real dangerous but they were real. They chose to be my friend and in many ways it was comforting to be around a group of guys who found something in me attractive in spite of my sinful nature. As far as life goes, they kept my head above water.

MY HEART IN A BAG

Dating is like two brain damaged people trying to teach each other math.

I would say I was about as ready for dating as Frosty the Snowman was to get in the greenhouse with Karen. First of all, most girls around my age didn't look like all those airbrushed girls I'd been staring at. There were a few but every guy in high school knew they were dating someone in college. Second, I was very aware I wasn't magazine quality myself. So with low self-esteem I began my climb up Everest already out of breath.

Everest- the mountain of love

I started wounded. The way pornography works is it seduces you with filet-minion but feeds you potted meat. I understood very late in life there is no substitute for the real thing. All the naked pictures in the world can't compete with the one true picture of female love for a man: a woman who loves him so much she will marry him.

Pornography gets you wound up to go get what you can't have, what you don't even really want. They say everybody wants to date a centerfold but marry Mother Teresa. I say who cares what we want, just help me understand what I really need. Pornography likes to lie to you about what you really need. At first I though I needed to have sex before I graduated high school.

My first job away from the farm was Burger King. There I suited up in brown polyester pants and a gold-checkered shirt, worked six hour shifts, got covered in grease, and fell in love with Tracey Lovelace. She had brown hair pulled back in a ponytail, beautiful brown eyes, and a nice figure. I'd stare at her and burn the fries.

40

After three months I got a different job at a dry cleaners but I didn't have the nerve to ask her out before I left so I figured I would just stalk her.

I memorized her schedule and proceeded to spend all my hard earned money at the Burger King drive-thru. Sometimes, when I didn't hear her voice on the menu speaker, I'd just drive off. I wasn't paying for the food. I was paying for Tracey.

After about a year (I was dedicated) we were spending her breaks together, enjoying conversation, when I heard the words I'd been dreaming of, *"Are you doing anything the weekend of my prom?"* I swallowed a chicken tender whole and said, *"No."* Then she said, *"Do you want to go to my prom?"* I almost stuck a straw up my nose and said, *"Yes."* For two whole seconds I celebrated the fact that we were boyfriend and girlfriend until I heard her say, *"Good, I have a friend who needs a date."*

For two seconds I thought I had reached the summit but then realized I was hallucinating at base camp. But all was not lost because I knew that birds of a feather flock together. Surely her friend was as pretty as she was. And if not, everybody who goes to the movies knows I would end up with Tracey by night's end. So I told her I would go.

I was informed a few days later my blind date would be wearing her grandmother's antique wedding dress. Still I thought, *"Who cares? I'll be with Tracey anyway."*

I showed up and sat on the couch with Tracey and her date (a freshman) waiting for my antique date to meet us in her living room. She floated down the stairs and I got up to meet her in the middle of the room were I discovered she smelled like mothballs. Everyone thought it was cute that I was getting emotional as my eyes started to water. I thought, *"Dang, I hope somebody smokes!"*

I was a very late bloomer mostly because it was easier to pop a tape in the VCR than deal with relationships. At the time I thought I was taking a short cut but later in life I understood my detours came to dead ends. I didn't even kiss a girl until the summer after high school. Her name was Cheryl.

She had a sexy nose like Sam on *Bewitched*, hazel eyes, strawberry blonde hair, and long smooth legs. She had hot hands too. Every time she touched me I started to sweat.

We were acquaintances in high school and I always viewed her as an out of my league sexy flirt. The night we graduated a good friend of mine invited me to join her boyfriend and her along with Cheryl to go hang out at Piney Lake. While Carol and Billy made out, me and Cheryl sat and talked, skipping rocks across the lake in the fog. The fog hid the fact that I was falling in love. I was sweating profusely.

The very next morning I left for freshmen orientation at the University of Oklahoma where I wanted to become a storm chaser and the big MF (master forecaster). The whole six hundred mile drive I thought about Cheryl.

We wound up dating that summer and of course I had no idea how to treat a girlfriend. The movies that had poisoned my mind taught me a girl's clothes were suppose to come off if she liked you. Cheryl spent most of her time successfully trying to fend off my sexual advances. The rest of the time we played miniature golf, went to the movies, and cuddled on the couch watching television, all fully clothed.

Saying good bye at night involved thirty minutes of leaning against each other, holding hands, and ten minutes of tongue wrestling but saying goodbye at the end of the summer involved something totally different.

Like Forest Gump talking about Bubba as he was dying in his arms, if I would have known this was the last time I'd see her I would have thought of something better to say. It wasn't the last time I saw her. It was just the last time the relationship was healthy enough to spend ten minutes French kissing.

Full closure came a year and a half later on Thanksgiving Day. I'd spent the summer working in a tile factory, earning money for school and getting angry with God while in a lovesick depression over her dating another guy. I chose Thanksgiving to say goodbye so she could remember me every time she ate turkey.

I pulled into her driveway and started beating on the door demanding to see her. I proceeded to tell her how worthless she was and how she never deserved anything I ever gave her and I told her I wanted it all back.

Crying she disappeared and a few minutes later produced jewelry and clothes. I looked in the bag and told her I also wanted the letters I had written her while I was away at college. Crying she ran and got those too. They were all neatly organized by date and held together with rubber bands almost like they had meant something to her.

With my heart in a bag, I jumped into my car and left black marks on the driveway. About a mile down the road I pulled over and cried so hard you could have seen through my shirt.

My philosophy was, knowing it was over, was better than not knowing if it would ever work out. I decided if I created a big enough scene she would never talk to me again. It worked, and I got my cushion back plus a hole to go with it. It's one of the dumbest things I ever did.

A few years ago I ran into her mother and asked how she was doing. Her mother said, *"She's having her ninetieth chemo treatment tomorrow."* She was fighting for her life. God probably knew I couldn't handle my wife battling cancer at the age of thirty.

Dating is like two brain damaged people trying to teach each other math. The formulas don't really work. It's more like art and most of the time it ends up looking like Picasso.

On the rebound, I headed for the highest concentration of babes I knew of: The cruising strip. We'd cruise five hours a night, seven days a week, honking when we saw a hot one and hiding when we saw

Cruising Strip- a loop you repeatedly drive in a town where you look for girls. Sorta like a slow Nascar Race

a warm one (not so hot). We thought if our car was clean and our music was loud it increased our chances for sex. We thought if we drove a convertible we could pick the girl we wanted. I bought one but guess it was the wrong color.

I think we were fishing without a hook. We were doing something wrong, but every once in a while we had one jump in our boat.

Her name was Alison and she was airbrushed. She had black hair, onyx eyes, a perfect tan, and a rich father. We met at 2am on a Tuesday. By Friday she pulled up to my car, gave me a hundred dollar bill, told me to go get a hotel room, winked and said she would see me at midnight after she got of work.

Her best friend saw me out around ten and asked to use the room for a little pre-party so I gave her the key. About ten minutes later Alison's sister pulled up crying. She said something had happened and she needed to know who Alison was staying with later. Since it appeared serious, I gave her the room number.

I waited until around 1am to make sure Alison was alone and pulled up at the motel sprayed with fresh deodorant and pickled in aftershave. I walked up to the door ready to cross the threshold of virginity into the land of Solomon and was pleasantly greeted by two girls and jerked into the room. I was nineteen and ten minutes away from statutory rape when God intervened.

They were crying hysterically and the room wreaked of beer. I waited for an explanation and through her sobs sixteen year old Alison said, "*My-my-D-Da-Daddy's out there.*"

Earlier that night when her sister pulled up crying he had been hiding in the back seat. Her father had forced her sister to betray her.

I was determined not to go back to "prison" and had no problem betraying people. So I grabbed the girls and shoved them out the door to face their fear of Alison's father and save my life. I locked it and put four inches of metal between me and the family feud that unfolded outside. I spent the rest of the night lying in a bed opposite my friend Scotty in a motel room that smelled like Budweiser. My gift with women almost got him killed one night.

Scotty was on the rebound like me, love sick over a girl named Suzie who lived in a town about twenty minutes away. Rusty and I thought we would give his love life a boost so we sent her flowers with an intoxicating love poem attached on his behalf.

The next night the three of us drove to Humboldt and I couldn't wait for Suzie to run up to Scotty and give him a reconciling French kiss. We stopped at Dairy Queen but Scotty, unaware of our scheme, was still depressed and chose to remain in the car and listen to music. Rusty and I walked away smiling at each other whistling, *"Here comes the bride"* and went inside to order.

We emerged to find the groom, Scotty, slumped in the front seat, face swollen, nose bleeding, mumbling expletives. We ran over and asked what happened. He said, *"I don't know what the #@%! they were talking about. Something about I better leave Suzie alone and stop sending #@%! roses!"* I looked at Rusty and we knew it was a secret we better keep.

When we got back to Jackson later that night Scotty assembled a small militia of about forty folks armed with baseball bats and chains. They all went back to Humboldt looking to rumble in the jungle. It taught me my romance skills were lethal like Romeo.

The youngest and shortest date I had was with a thirteen-year-old girl when I was almost twenty. Her brother told me she was sixteen. She was drunk when I picked her up and she wanted to smoke. Although I liked the smell, I told her not in my car. She wanted to drink. I told her she was already drunk. She wanted to eat. I told her she would throw up. She wanted to change my radio station. I told her to get out. I left her standing at a red light. You don't mess with a man's radio.

I had a night class with a forty-five year old woman. I'd walk her out to her car every night because the parking lot wasn't safe. We hit it off immediately and one night while walking her to her car she said, *"Come here I want to show you something."*

In her hand was a picture of a seventeen-year-old girl named Kathy, her daughter. She asked me what I thought and I told her she was pretty. *"Well good,"* she said. *"You can come over on Sunday to meet her."* We dated a while but Kathy always thought she was too wild for me. I laugh about that now.

Perhaps the girl I enjoyed dating the most was a girl who cut my hair. Unfortunately she was married. Even worse, I didn't know it at the time.

She seemed to pay special attention to my shoulders while sculpting my head. A clue so obvious even I could tell she loved me. I checked for a ring and didn't see one so I decided to send her flowers.

I got a call later that evening from the florist telling me she was there with a cop demanding to know who had sent them. I had sent the flowers anonymously and playfully signed the card, "*Guess Who?*" They said she was causing a scene and needed to tell her it was me who sent them to get rid of her. I said, "*Better yet, put her on the phone.*" We talked about an hour.

Realizing things were going well, I asked, "*Can I have your number and call you at home later?*" She said, "*No. But we can go to lunch tomorrow!*"

Because of hindsight I know she didn't give me her number because her husband might have answered the phone. Her cop friend was there to pressure the florist into coughing up information because Tammy couldn't go home and thank her husband for flowers he hadn't sent nor could she go home and not thank him for flowers he had sent. She had a dilemma and so did I.

Where do you take a cute strawberry blonde on the first date? I don't even remember where we went but I guess it was a good choice because a few weeks later we were planning a day trip to Nashville.

In order to get the day off I had to get dramatic. I told my boss a small white lie. I told him Tammy and I needed to go to Nashville to talk a friend out of having an abortion. It was a life and death situation so he had to let me go.

It snowed big, heavy, wet flakes all the way to Nashville. It looked a lot like our gingerbread house but I didn't understand the omen. I looked over at my sexy new girl and pretended I was in a music video as we listened to Paula Abdul on CD.

We got to Nashville and ate at a quaint, historic restaurant and had a caricature drawn before we went to tour the Opryland Hotel. Later at Opryland we were walking around all romantic like (this is where you put your hands in each other's back pocket) when she pulled me into a Victoria Secret store. She picked a few things out and we headed for home but not before having a snowball fight in the parking lot.

Back at her apartment (she had moved in with a friend) we sat down to watch TV when she looked over at me and said, *"I'm going to slip into something more comfortable."* Just as my mind wandered into the land of Solomon, God called.

It wasn't really God but then again probably was. **Mojo**- sex drive
It was my mother on the phone. Several hours earlier she had called my work looking for me. My confused boss had told her my girlfriend and I had gone to see about an abortion. Nothing in the world zaps your mojo like the angry voice of your mother. I went home still a virgin.

So somehow I managed to crawl through my underage years chaste but broken hearted. I've dated a few women since then. Some of them I've really liked but our calculators always malfunctioned. It's amazing how much of your heart you put into people when you really like them. It is also amazing how heavy that bag gets in just a short period of time.

I'm not trying to trivialize this rebellious time in my life by laughing about it. I laugh about it so I don't cry. It was a time in life when rejection was difficult and deeply felt. I'm very fortunate I didn't get a girl "looking for love" pregnant with my mojo. I'm also no longer angry at God about helping me keep something my wife might appreciate one day. I'm not a virgin because I was strong, brave, or even less brain damaged than my sexually active friends. I believe I'm a virgin because of two reasons: the prayers of my church and family, and the fact that God still makes house calls.

STICKY CARDBOARD
*I was unemployed, dropping out of college
and had just totaled my convertible.*

I remember at the age of seven when I was with my family at a theme park on a hot summer day. I'd spent four hours pulling on my Mom's shirt begging for a dollar to buy a stick of cotton candy. Like Chinese water torture dripping on her forehead, my little tugging hand eventually worked its magic. I grabbed the dollar and ran back to the nearest cart.

I had one eye on the man wrapping God's hair around the cardboard as I wondered how I could grow up and get a good job like that. My other eye was still on my parents who were slipping farther and farther away.

I'd been lost before at the Memphis fair. I was rescued by gentle, old people who smelled like baby powder and fed me ice cream until my parents showed up. But for some reason, that has never made sense, I didn't want to repeat the incident.

Finally I pushed the dollar into the vendors hand, grabbed my cotton candy, thought, *"Man I just ripped you off"* and ran to catch up with my family. Out of breath, I strategically placed myself on the opposing side of my sisters, smirked at them, and turned to take a bite of sugar heaven. I found myself staring at a sticky piece of cardboard. It had melted. Tears came instantly.

At the age of twenty-one I found myself thinking hard about sticky cardboard, magazines in calf barns, and what it felt like to try to breathe unassisted on the mountain of love. I was unemployed, dropping out of college, and had just totaled my convertible. It was the wrong color anyway.

For the past two years I had distanced myself from church and all those candy coated stories because, to be honest, they didn't hold up to my real life experiences. Yet for some reason the verses Brenda Knipper packed into my head during Sunday night Bible drills haunted me, proving the word of God does not return void.[1] Tired and partially confused, I found myself sitting in a church pew again.

The first thing I thought would break the ice was a public confession, or at least my version of one. As part of a youth service, I got up and told everyone I had heard from God. I told them I was tired of running and in-between sobs apologized for my ten thousand dollar investment in a car radio, for getting angry at God and for embarrassing my family by going to "prison." I left the stealing and X-rated parts out. It was church not an AA meeting.

I wish it would have been an AA meeting, because maybe I would have followed everyone else's example and told the whole truth. I didn't drink but sometimes I think if I would have I might have been a part of a group of souls who are notorious for listening and being seasoned enough to handle the truth.

However, the candy coated version of my life was convincing enough that I was appointed the position of part time youth pastor. Now instead of trying to figure it out for myself, I had to figure it out for a whole bunch of other inexperienced climbers. I was no Edmund Hillary. I was still trying to learn how to turn on my oxygen tank. In many ways, I was still just a boy- a boy named Hammer.

> *Edmund Hillary-* legendary mountain climber who would summit mountains without the aid of oxygen bottles

1. Isaiah 55:11

51

For the rest of this story, go to:
www.greenfrogcoffeeco.com

"Love Him with all your devotion, set your thoughts on Him, and give Him the use of your hands. Then love those around you as if you shared the same heart."

Mark 12:30-31